914.9503
R   Rice, T.A.T.
c.3

        Byzantium

LONG TERM LOAN SUBJECT TO RECALL	DATE DUE	

Byzantium

The colorful story of Byzantium, too little known to most American readers, begins with the decline of the old Roman Empire, which had become impossibly vast to govern. It stretched from Britain to Africa. In AD 324 Rome was divided into two halves, each with its own Emperor – the Emperor in the West and the Emperor in the East. The first Emperor in the East, Constantine the Great, founded his new capital overlooking the Bosporus Strait, where Istanbul stands in Turkey today. The new city of Byzantium, or Constantinople as it was often called, became the hub of a great multi-racial Christian civilization which lasted more than a thousand years, and left a great heritage of things Byzantine in many areas of European culture.

In this introduction to Byzantium, the author has picked out the main landmarks: the founding of Byzantium and the reign of Constantine, the Golden Age of Justinian the Great and Theodora, the Iconoclast Controversy, and the Four Crusades. Through these topics, she illuminates family life, monastic life and the influence of religion, art and scholarship, warfare, and the imperial dynasties, and shows how the peoples and culture of Byzantium flourished while Europe was plunged in a Dark Age.

The text is fully illustrated with photographs, line drawings and maps.

Other books for the Young Historian, uniform with this volume

THE YOUNG HISTORIAN BOOKS   *Edited by Patrick Rooke*

Byzantium

TAMARA TALBOT RICE

DRAWINGS BY MARGARET SCOTT

THE JOHN DAY COMPANY
New York

To May Gilchrist
devoted friend and teacher

Contents

List of Illustrations

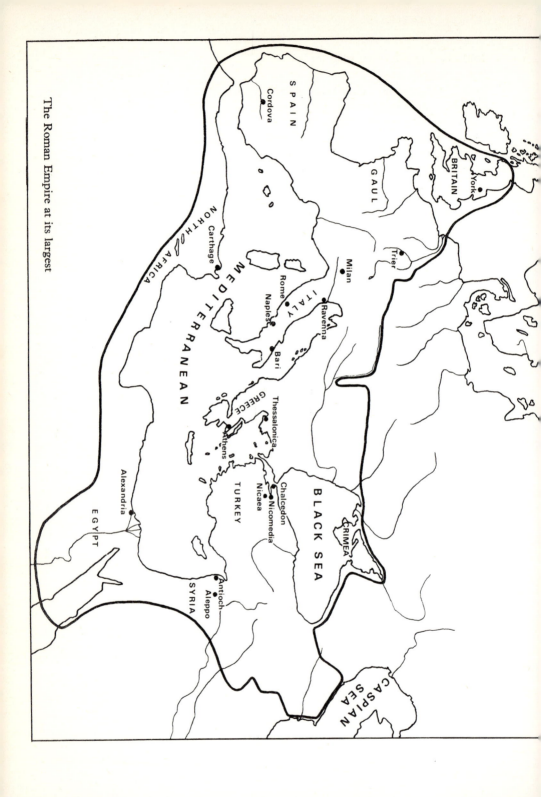

The Roman Empire at its largest

CHAPTER ONE

From Rome to Byzantium

TODAY, standing astride the Bosporus, the ancient city of Istanbul is a meeting point of west and east, Europeans and Asians, Christians and Turks. Over a thousand years ago, this same city was called Byzantium, or Constantinople after its founder, Constantine the Great; this was the capital of the Byzantine Empire. In this book we will discover how this great empire grew up out of the declining Roman world, and became the focal point of a great new Christian civilization.

With Italy forming its core, the immense Roman Empire stretched so far to the west that it included England, Gaul, and Spain, while to the southeast of Italy the vast area which is divided today among Greece, Turkey, Syria, and Israel belonged to it; so did Egypt and the Mediterranean fringe of North Africa. Yet even though the Romans were such successful empire builders, their territory became too large and unwieldy to administer. Rome's greatness began to decline, but its collapse was delayed by one man's energy and foresight – Constantine the Great. By transforming the Roman into the Byzantine Empire he revived its flagging energy and spirit. To see how he did so we must glance back to the closing years of the pre-Christian Era, to a time when Rome's greatness seemed undiminished, yet when it had in reality started on a course of decline.

Rome had been a great power for some eight centuries before it began to lose its grip. Some farsighted men became aware of this during the opening centuries of the Christian Era. They urged reform but disagreed about what should be done. Some believed that a more autocratic form of government was necessary if Rome's greatness was to be restored; others maintained that it would be better to divide the empire into regions which could be governed from local centers; still others suggested that their capital should be

Rome's problems

moved from Rome to some other town, one where the corruption of the old city could be avoided. This last group thought that the government would adjust itself sooner in a new town to modern needs and conditions and that it would be easier to control such a large empire and the many different peoples it contained from a more conveniently placed capital. Some Romans were impressed by the profound respect with which the Persians, though they were Rome's most dangerous rivals, treated their kings, and it was largely due to them that, in the first century after Christ, the Roman Emperor Augustus was able to proclaim himself *Divi Filius* (Son of God). Partly as a result of this, by the third century, Emperor Diocletian (284 – 305) had come to believe that a Roman emperor possessed a degree of divinity which entitled him to unrestricted control over his people. He demanded that right for himself and for the emperors who were to reign after him, and gave this privilege visible form by legally restricting the wearing of purple-colored stuffs to members of the imperial family. He chose purple because the dye was scarce and expensive, for it could be obtained only by using the rare murex shell.

Rome's decline   Rome had grown steadily weaker since the death of Emperor Augustus, and Diocletian was convinced that drastic changes were needed. One of his reforms was to move his capital from Rome to Nicomedia, the town in Asian Turkey which is now known to us as Izmit. He also attempted to restore the people's trust in their pagan gods by resisting Christianity as firmly and energetically as possible. Although he ruled his empire as a complete autocrat, Diocletian still had to split up the country, so that the administrative duties might be shared. He was not the first Roman ruler to believe that constitutional changes had become necessary. Others before him had hoped to improve conditions within the empire by sharing their duties with one or more co-rulers. Diocletian preferred to make use of the collegiate system in place of co-rulership. It involved dividing the empire not only between himself and his co-ruler, but also among two others. Each of the latter was to be invested with the title of *caesar* and to be promoted later to the rank of *augustus;* each was to become the virtual ruler of his area. One, Constantius, was the father of Constantine, the man who was to found the

Byzantine Empire. He was given Spain, Gaul and Britain, with the town of Trier situated just north of the Rhine as his capital. The system gave good results, but not sufficiently so to inject new life and energy into the flagging empire.

Constantius was a warmhearted man of upright character. *Constantius* When young, he had married Helena, thought by some to have been an English princess, perhaps even a daughter of the legendary King Cole of Colchester of nursery rhyme fame, but most scholars think that her father was an inn-keeper at Nicomedia. They called their son Constantine. Though their marriage is thought to have been happy, Diocletian obliged Constantius to divorce Helena when he became heir to the northern section of the empire and to marry instead a daughter of his adopted father the Emperor Maximilian. Constantine was twenty years old at the time. He was a member of Diocletian's court, and although he remained on good and close terms with his parents, he stayed with Diocletian for several years more, probably gaining much valuable experience in politics and the art of governing while there. Nothing is known of Helena's life following her divorce beyond the fact that she became a Christian and that she went on a pilgrimage to the Holy Land. The Greeks believe that she discovered the True Cross there and brought it back with her to Constantinople, and for this reason, and also perhaps because of the influence she may have exercised over Constantine, she was made a saint of the Eastern Church. As governor of Gaul and Britain, Constantius proved lenient to Christians, allowing them to practice their religion, a policy which seems to have recommended itself to his son, Constantine.

Though Constantine admired Diocletian's gifts as a statesman and shared many of his opinions, he noted with concern that the Roman Empire continued to decline. He came to feel that its division among several rulers had made things worse rather than better. On inheriting the governor-ship of Spain, Gaul, and Britain at his father's death in 306, he therefore set out to control the whole empire. Time was to show that he too believed in the divinity of kings and shared Diocletian's faith in the value of autocracy.

It took Constantine eighteen years to achieve his ambition. He became emperor in 324, and within a matter of 11

weeks he informed the nation that he had decided to move his capital out of Rome. There were many ancient towns from which Constantine could have chosen a new capital. Like Diocletian, he could have settled on Nicomedia, or like Galerius, he could have decided on Thessalonica; he could have picked a famous ancient town such as Alexandria or Antioch, both great commercial centers; Athens, with a long history behind it, was another possibility. But he preferred to make a clean break with the past. In November, 324, he announced his decision to establish his capital in the obscure town of Byzantium, which occupied a small, triangular-shaped promontory of land jutting out toward Asia Minor at the northern end of the Sea of Marmora; it is now known as Istanbul.

The founding of Byzantium   Although Byzantium was a small and little-known townlet at the time, it was far from being young, for it had been founded as far back as the seventh century BC by a group of Greeks from the city of Megara in Greece. Before these pioneers left their homes in search of fame and fortune, their leader, a man called Byzas, had made a point of consulting their local oracle. In the mysterious manner of all oracles it told them to settle "opposite the city of the blind." Sorely puzzled, the Megarians set out on their expedition and at last reached a small promontory where the Sea of Marmora merges with the Bosporus. Though they were at first attracted to it by its beauty, they quickly noticed the site's geographical advantages, for it was triangular in shape, bordered by water along its two longer sides. Then, as they looked across the narrow strip of sea separating them from Asia, they saw the town of Chalcedon spread out on the opposite shore. They realized that Chalcedon's position was not nearly as promising from either a commercial or a defensive point of view; they understood then the meaning of the oracle's words; Chalcedon was to be recognized as the town of the blind, because its inhabitants had not appreciated the advantages of the other site. The explorers therefore decided to build their town on the promontory – on the site of present-day Istanbul – and to call it Byzantium in honor of their leader.

The Megarians and their descendants did not grow wealthy in Byzantium, but Constantine was as quick as they had been in realizing that the town's position could not

The Golden Horn

Map showing Constantinople's position on the fringe of Europe

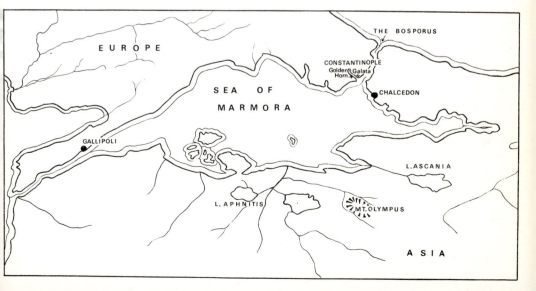

be bettered. To its north an inlet of the sea formed such a splendid natural harbor that the Byzantines were to lose little time before naming it the Golden Horn. Ships sailing from it could pass through the Bosporus and, on entering the Black Sea, either sail westward to the ports serving central Europe or head for the Crimea for those connecting with the Slavonic hinterland and with Scandinavia; they could equally well turn eastward, on entering the Black Sea, for those ports which handled the Caucasian trade, and which linked up with the overland routes connecting them with such rich and mysterious countries as India and China and also with central Asia. Overland routes from western Europe that already existed could also easily be extended to Byzantium, where travelers had only to cross a narrow strip of the Sea of Marmora in order to reach Asia Minor; from there they could travel on either to Asia or to Africa.

Constantine's plans for Byzantium When Constantine chose Byzantium as his capital, the city was too small and ill equipped for the purpose. Undismayed, he drew up a list of the buildings which were essential to him and gave orders for these to be built as quickly as possible. They included a palace, a forum, a hippodrome, some government departments, and the houses which his courtiers and officials would need. He personally traced the lines of the town's new boundaries; they were to be used for the foundations of a great wall starting from shore to shore across the peninsula and strengthened at regular intervals by towers; at the same time seawalls were built along the seashore. They were to defend his future capital from enemy attacks, whether from land or from sea.

Constantine's attitude to Christianity While the builders were carrying out Constantine's instructions, the emperor turned his attention to affairs of state and especially to the religious situation. During the centuries since Christ's Crucifixion, Christianity had gained a great many converts and was steadily adding to the number. In 311 AD Galerius had found it necessary to grant certain concessions to the Christians. In 313, when in Milan, Constantine had gone further, for he had passed a law allowing Christians freely to practice their religion. By then it would not have been politically wise to do otherwise, but there was no immediate need for Constantine to have done anything else to help the Christians. Nevertheless, he con-

The sea walls of Constantinople. They were built by Constantine the Great

tinued to protect and support them, and in 324 he included a cathedral among the buildings that he regarded as essential in his future capital. He was to dedicate it to Hagia Sophia, meaning the Divine or Holy Wisdom.

It was to prove unfortunate for Christendom that even by Constantine's day its doctrine was already being interpreted slightly differently by converts living in the western or European section of the Roman Empire from those living in its eastern regions. The result was to split the Church in two. The western part, based in Rome and headed by the Pope, was to develop into the Roman Catholic Church, while the eastern was soon to be directed by the Patriarch of Constantinople and to become the Eastern or Orthodox Church; the Cathedral of Hagia Sophia filled the same place there as St. Peter's Cathedral in Rome later did in the west. Constantine did not officially become a Christian till he was on the point of death, yet as soon as he became emperor, he openly and warmly upheld the Christian Church. He had probably decided to do so some ten years earlier when he had a strange revelation.

The two branches of Christianity

15

It happened, so it is thought, on an October night in the year 311, when Constantine was encamped with his army on the outskirts of Rome, waiting to give battle to Maxentius. As he sat in the entrance to his tent, perhaps pondering on the outcome of the battle on which his future depended, he saw the sun appear in the night sky. In antiquity the sun had been regarded as the emblem of the sun-god, Apollo, and Rome's Caesars, including Constantine, had therefore adopted the sun as their sign or crest. Constantine now saw, silhouetted against its rays, a great golden standard with a cross set on its tip. Two purple streamers shot with gold and decorated with sparkling jewels were attached to each arm of the cross; it also carried a gold coronet which displayed another cross, its arms forming the Greek letters *chi rho*, standing for the first letters of Christ's name in Greek X P, Khi R. Some accounts of the event add that the words *hoc vices* (By this conquer) also appeared in the sky. Constantine thought that he also heard a voice telling him to instruct his men to paint the *chi rho* on their shields before engaging Maxentius in battle. At first Constantine doubted his vision, thinking that he had either dreamed or imagined it, but as the thought flashed across his mind, Christ appeared before him, telling him that he was also to display the initials on his personal standard. Constantine did as he had been instructed and defeated Maxentius.

Scarcely had the Romans got used to the idea that their town was no longer to be the empire's capital than they found that Constantine intended to encourage the Christians by openly declaring himself the protector of their church. By doing so, he made Christianity supreme, even though it did not become the empire's official religion till Emperor Theodosius I (379 – 95) proclaimed it so, banning all pagan practices and destroying all pagan temples. In addition to his secular role as head of the state, Constantine assumed that of head of the Church. He insisted on being recognized as Christ's vicar on earth. All the emperors who followed him on the Byzantine throne were to claim and to hold both ranks. All believed as firmly as Constantine had done in the divine right of kings and in their personal right to combine the duties of head of the state with those of head of the church. The Byzantine people never challenged these claims; indeed, they believed that because the emperors had succeeded the earlier Caesars as supreme heads of the Roman Empire and because each had also become Christ's vicar on earth, each was the only ruler in the world who was entitled to use the title of emperor. They agreed with the emperors in expecting lesser sovereigns to content themselves with the title of king.

As the Church's protector, Constantine summoned the first of many Councils of the Church. It met at Nicaea in the year 325 with Constantine in the chair. Later emperors too made a point of presiding at such Councils. There were many details both in the Church's ritual and in its understanding of religious texts which needed to be discussed at the Council of 325. The Council also had to define the position of the two branches of the Church, their exact relationship to each other, and the rank of their respective primates. All this proved exceedingly difficult to settle. After lengthy discussions it was agreed that the Pope of Rome should take precedence over the Patriarch of the Eastern Church because his see was the older of the two, but that both should nevertheless rank as equals. The decision was an impossible one to apply in practice, and the question of whether the Pope was more important than the Patriarch was never satisfactorily settled. Each longed to see his office recognized as the senior; different popes and patriarchs quarreled violently about this matter; in the eighth century Pope Gregory III was to insist on his right to act independently of the emperor when he thought fit, a decision which resulted in the popes becoming more influential in the Western world and the patriarchs more so in the Eastern.

The two branches of the Church

Constantine's championship of Christianity marked the beginning of a new era in the history of Europe. The Christian doctrine did much to improve the position of women and led people to regard the family in a new light. A more compassionate attitude taught people to be considerate and to examine their own conduct and to distinguish between right and wrong. This in its turn introduced charity into a world which had sadly lacked it. Many of the customs which still form the basis of our own lives were first recognized as desirable in Constantine's day.

It took only six years to complete all the buildings which

B

Constantine needed in Byzantium to enable him to establish his capital there. On May 15, 330, he was at last able to proclaim Byzantium his capital. Though he renamed it Constantinople, the city of Constantine, the town's older name did not die out; instead, it came to be used to describe the eastern part of the Roman Empire as a whole. Yet the people who moved from Rome to live in Constantinople seldom called it by its new name; they generally referred to it as the New Rome. That name took root in Anatolia, and even today peasants living in remote areas of Asiatic Turkey continue to speak of Europe as Rum, the name which their ancestors applied centuries ago to the Roman Empire as a whole.

The new capital　　Although Constantine set out to make a fresh start in Constantinople, he rebuilt the city on Roman lines. He gave it the public buildings which were essential to Rome; he gave it straight streets intersecting at right angles, as in Rome. He lined these streets with houses, the best of which, as at Ostia, near Rome, were two stories high and had their owner's names carved on their fronts. The new main street, the Mese, ran as straight as possible from the city's main gate to its very heart. The gate that survives today was erected by Emperor Theodosius around the year 400; though built of marble, it came to be called the Golden Gate because it was faced with copper sheeting which shone in the sunlight like gold; it was used only on ceremonial occasions. The Mese divided the town into two almost equal parts and led to the Cathedral of Hagia Sophia on the way passing close to the hippodrome. Constantine laid out a great square between the cathedral and the hippodrome, calling it the Augustaion in honor of his mother, the Augusta Helena. He placed columns along its sides and a statue of his mother at its center. He also marked the start of the Mese with a column, setting it opposite the main gate leading to his palace. The column was known as the Milium, for like a similar one in Rome, it had the distances to various parts of the empire cut on it. The houses bordering the Mese were arcaded; many had shops at street level with, here and there, a statue adorning the arcade. There was a forum not far from Hagia Sophia named after Constantine and later the Forum of Theodosius, the Forum Tauri, and

18

The Golden Gate, Constantinople. It was used by the emperors on ceremonial occasions

forums called after the emperors Arcadius and Anastasius were laid out at points close to the Mese. Geography joined hands with architecture to increase Constantinople's resemblance to Rome, for each town contained seven hills.

The inhabitants of Byzas' town were Greeks, descendants of the Megarians who had founded it. They spoke Greek and read Greek books, their education followed the Greek system, they thought like the Greeks and worshiped the same gods as the Greeks, yet their tastes and ideas had been influenced by their Eastern neighbors, especially by the Syrian merchants whom they often met. The Christians among them were also often influenced by Egypt's Christian communities. Yet it does not seem to have occurred to Constantine to look to the local Greeks for the officials he needed in his new capital. Instead, he insisted on Romans coming to serve there, expecting them to abandon their homes and friends in Rome to live and work in Constantinople as courtiers and administrators. Most were very reluctant to come to a new and remote city lacking most of Rome's attractions. Constantine had to persuade, even to order, them to uproot themselves with their families, ser- 19

Constantinople's inhabitants

The Byzantines never ceased to delight in the culture of ancient Greece and often decorated secular objects, such as this fifth century glass bucket, with mythological scenes

vants, and household goods to settle in the new capital. They came wearing their togas, speaking Latin, determined to bring up their children in the Roman manner and to continue to live as they had done in Rome. As a result, Constantinople acquired a mixed, Romano-Greek population.

Language problem and social structure Although the Roman community was very much smaller than the native Greek one, it was, at any rate at first, the more important, for it gave the emperor his courtiers, ministers, and officials. Latin became Byzantium's official language, and it took the Greeks some three centuries to get the situation reversed; not until the reign of Emperor Heraclius (610-41) was Greek proclaimed the official language. Almost at once Latin fell out of use and was quickly forgotten by all but a small number of scholars. By then, however, Rome had made its own great contribution to Byzantium's culture. The clear-cut character of Byzantium's social structure, where each class was sharply distinguished from the others, reflects the Roman love of clarity and precision. It can be compared to a pyramid, with

20

the emperor forming its summit and the Patriarch of Constantinople serving as his pedestal. The next section was made up of the imperial family, followed by the emperor's bodyguard, his courtiers, his ministers, and the nation's leading churchmen; the civil servants and fighting services came next, with scholars, artists, merchants, and technicians ranking just below. Smaller tradesmen and master crafts-men, as well as the members of the professional guilds, craftsmen, manual workers, and peasants, came next, while slaves formed the pyramid's base. Although the rights of each group were carefully regulated and defined by law, the system, while leaving people free within their groups, never-theless turned the free population into the emperor's sub-jects, instead of granting them, as Rome had first done, the privileges of citizenship. It was possible for a person to become a member of a higher social class than the one of his birth by either marriage or ability, but the whole population was also strictly controlled by the Church.

The Byzantines readily accepted the new order introduced by Constantine and their faith in Christianity was so great that they willingly obeyed the Church's rule. They hoped that their attempts to live as good Christians would entitle them to enter paradise at death. Their attitude to their government was more complicated. At times they did not hesitate to express their feelings by rioting. If an emperor displeased them, they paid no attention to his high rank and did not hesitate to depose him; torture, humiliation, even death might be his fate. They believed that God sometimes imposed a bad emperor on them as a punishment for their sins, but that He allowed them to rebel when the punishment had run its course.

In addition to bringing his courtiers and officials from *The Senate* Rome, Constantine provided Byzantium with a Senate of the Roman type. To begin with, its members were former Senators of Rome, but their place was gradually filled by men of local birth, though these still belonged to the families which had come to Constantinople from Rome. Constanti-nople's Senators were to be entitled to the same privileges as Roman ones, but by the fourth century the latter had lost so many of their earlier rights that those of Constantinople never acquired them. Rome's Senate had once ruled the 21

An ivory plaque of the Empress Ariadne. At the death of her husband, Zeno, in 491 she chose Anastasius I to succeed him as emperor, by becoming his wife.

22

empire, but that of Constantinople never came near to doing so, for Constantine and his successors reserved that right for themselves and their Cabinet. Constantine's Cabinet was a very small one; he himself chose its members, selecting them from the highest officers of state, but Senators with special knowledge or experience could be called to attend a meeting dealing with some matter on which they could give useful advice.

There were times when the Senate was able to play a more active part in politics than at others, and there was one situation when the Senate was entitled to take charge and, after consulting the senior commanders of the army and navy, to impose its wish. This happened when an emperor died. Though the ancient Roman tradition of an elected consul or ruler had fallen out of use in Rome well before Constantine's reign, so much importance continued to be attached to the idea that, at any rate to begin with, the crown was not regarded as hereditary in Byzantium. Nevertheless, emperors were entitled to chose and to nominate their successors, and many an aging or ill emperor made use of that right. If an emperor died without having done so, his widow or a member of his immediate family was entitled to choose the next emperor, but that person had to obtain the Senate's assent before the nomination became valid. When there was no relative who could act on behalf of the late emperor or when a revolution had deprived his relations of the right to do so, it fell to the Senate to elect the ruler.

At first Byzantium's emperors were not crowned on coming to power. Instead the office was conferred on them at a ceremony dating back to the time when Rome's rulers were indeed elected by the city's freemen. The emperor was placed on a shield and raised on it high above the heads of the assembled regiments and people. The crowd's cheers indicated their willingness to accept him as their emperor. However, the Patriarch of Constantinople became so important a figure within fifty years of the adoption of Christianity as Byzantium's official religion that, when he became emperor in 457, Leo I decided to have the crown conferred upon him at a religious ceremony. His coronation took place in the Cathedral of Hagia Sophia with the Patriarch of Constantinople officiating. In the course of the service it was

Succession to the throne

23

The crest of the emperors of Byzantium

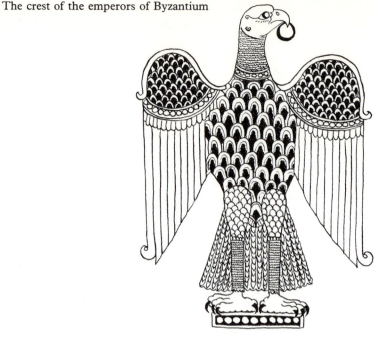

The shapes of the imperial crowns varied slightly with each century. These were worn by Constantine IX and the Empress Zoe early in the eleventh century

the Patriarch who placed the crown on the emperor's head. From then onward Byzantium's rulers were always crowned in Hagia Sophia. The ceremony followed the lines which had been worked out for Leo I's coronation. Many of its features were adopted in the ninth century by Europe's kings for their own coronations; some even found their way into the English coronation service and remain in force to this day. Since the emperors generally chose one of their sons to succeed them, the hereditary principle was gradually introduced into Byzantium, but it never became necessary for the crown to pass to the emperor's eldest son; the sovereign could, if he wished, choose a younger son to succeed him.

When Greek replaced Latin as the country's official language, the habit of referring to the ruler by the Latin title of *emperor* was replaced by the Greek form of *basileus*, but at the same time the emperors adopted the Roman eagle as their crest. It had been displayed by Rome's legionaries on their standards centuries earlier, at a time when the eagle was associated with Jupiter, the greatest of the pagan gods.

24

The Byzantine emperors chose it to serve as the symbol of their might; first, they showed it as a single-headed bird; later, probably in the fourteenth century, they gave it a second head in order to distinguish it from the one which the emperors of Germany had, to their intense annoyance, decided to use as their crest.

Constantine's reforms had a bracing effect, even though the choice of a capital poised on the edge of Asia tended to divert attention from the western to the eastern provinces. By doing so, it helped divide the empire into two sections. The division was underlined by Constantine, who, even though he had spent so much of his life trying to bring the whole empire under the control of a single ruler, yet, shortly before his death, revived the system of co-rulership. He may have done so because he realized that the empire was too unwieldy as a single unit, but it seems more probable that he acted out of love for his sons in the hope of ending their jealousies. Whatever the reason, he made the mistake of dividing the empire among his three sons. This emphasized the division between East and West without bringing his sons to reason. Their quarrel over the throne became so violent that they decided to fight the issue out. The death of young Constantine within a few months of his father led the two surviving brothers to share the empire; its division gained greater importance from the fact that the Church was split into an eastern and a western branch. Constantine the Great's plan for a strong, vital, and united empire was killed. Nevertheless, Constantine had unknowingly created a new country, that of Byzantium. It was the first to base its existence on Christian principles while continuing to claim precedence over all other powers. As Byzantium it was to enjoy great commercial prosperity, to win many battle honors, but above all, it was to provide the world with a vital Christian culture on which Western Europe's civilization was largely based. These achievements were quickly appreciated by the Byzantines, who were among the first to confer the title of Great on their first emperor – a verdict which later historians have confirmed.

Division of the empire

CHAPTER TWO

The Age of Justinian the Great

MANY of the emperors who followed Constantine the Great as ruler of Byzantium shared his longing to see the empire made whole again, but like him, they generally found that they were obliged to deal with one consisting of two sections. Some emperors went to war in order to join both parts together and occasionally succeeded in doing so for a short time.

The Barbarian threat

Their task was made more difficult by the sudden arrival on their country's western and northern borders of several groups of fierce and primitive people, who, to their surprise, dared to pit their strength against that of Byzantium. The Goths were among the first to do so, having migrated from their north European homelands to occupy southern Russia and parts of central Europe. They were soon in their turn overrun by the even fiercer and more terrifying Asian Huns. The death of Attila, leader of the Huns, in 454 saved them and also Western Europe from death and desolation, for Attila's soldiers plundered so savagely that it was said that land where they grazed their horses became a desert.

When the Huns disappeared, the Goths began to threaten Byzantium. There were so many of them that they broke into two groups. One called itself the Ostrogoth, the other the Visigoth. By 476 Odoacer, King of the Ostrogoths, had captured most of Italy, while Gaul and Spain had fallen to the Visigoths. At much the same time another group of nomads, known as the Vandals, reached Byzantium's European borders and soon captured its northwestern and north African provinces with the exception of Greece and the northern Balkans. They then proceeded to turn much of the conquered territory into a kingdom of their own. Like the Greeks and the Romans before them, the Byzantines had been in the habit of dismissing nomadic communities such as these as barbarians. Their growing importance not only strained Byzantium's military resources, but also hurt its pride.

In the year 527 the Byzantine throne passed to Justinian, perhaps the most famous man in all Byzantine history. The son of a poor Macedonian peasant, he was to become a great historical figure and was certainly a remarkable, and outstanding emperor. Justinian was born in Illyria, and Latin was therefore his mother tongue. Although he received little education as a child, he later learned to speak Greek no less well than Latin, and he grew up to be one of the most learned men of his age. Justinian had an uncle, called Justin, who had exchanged a peasant's life for a soldier's. His courage and intelligence had been quickly appreciated in the Byzantine army, and he rapidly received promotion. He continued to distinguish himself and was again rewarded. His rise to senior rank was rapid. By 518 his reputation stood so high that at the death of Emperor Anastasius I, Justin was chosen to succeed him.

The Emperor Justinian

Although Justin was a brilliant soldier, he was the first to realize that his limited schooling had not fitted him for the throne. By then, however, Justinian had given himself a good education. He had been drawn to learning from early boyhood and had not been content merely to admire it from afar. He had studied and become a well-informed, clear-thinking and cultivated person. Wisely, Justin took him on as his private secretary and assistant. Justinian proved loyal and efficient, as well as a good judge of men and a sincere patriot. Justin realized that he would make a good ruler and appointed him his successor. His judgement was borne out by later events, for Justinian is among the very small number of rulers who have had the title of Great conferred on them by historians.

Like many of those who delight in their country's reputation, Justinian looked back admiringly to the period of Rome's greatness and longed to see it revived. Even when his uncle's assistant, he had planned and worked for the empire's unity regardless of the fact that the barbarians were at that very time conquering large areas of Italy. His greatest shortcoming lay in his inability to realize that a new Europe was coming into being, that the change in outlook

Justinian's military aims

there could not be disregarded. He failed to understand that the nationalist spirit behind these movements would eventually alter the patterns on his map. On becoming emperor, Justinian therefore placed the task of uniting the empire at the head of the aims which he set himself. He wanted the impossible, for Europe was on the verge of splitting up into countries, and the system he hoped to see restored was outdated. The situation was made more difficult for him by the jealousies and real religious differences between the Pope and his Catholic followers and the Patriarch of Constantinople and his Orthodox congregations.

Persia, enemy of Byzantium   Although the situation in Europe made it necessary for the emperors to keep large armies there, often even to send them into battle, none of their Western enemies could at this date have planned to conquer Byzantium; they could hope for little beyond the conquest of Italy and the Balkans. In the East, however, it was different; Persia was anxious to destroy Byzantium. Persia and Rome had been rivals for centuries. Persia's new rulers, kings of the Sassanian Dynasty, wished to revive the glory Persia had enjoyed in earlier times. In order to do so, they were bent on winning back the territories which had once belonged to Persia, but which had been lost to the Romans many years earlier. The Sassanians were daring and brave. They were also keen sportsmen, and in peacetime they devoted their leisure to playing polo, hunting, and hawking. Justinian ought perhaps to have sent the bulk of his army to fight the Persians with a view to reaching a permanent settlement of the Eastern problem, but he was so anxious to win Italy back that he hoped to obtain a seven-year truce from the Persians. He entered into peace talks with them, but these made such slow progress that it was not until five years had been spent in difficult negotiations that he obtained a five-year truce in return for a yearly payment. The emperor was satisfied with this, for in five years he might be able to reconquer the empire's former territories in Italy.

The campaigns of Belisarius and Narses   Two extremely able and experienced generals had by then given Justinian ample proof of their loyalty. One was called Belisarius, the other Narses. Justinian unhesitatingly appointed Belisarius to command the army of 18,000 men which was to open the campaign by winning back North

Africa for him. Belisarius struck at the Vandals in 533. Within a year he had retaken North Africa, and although guerrilla fighting continued on and off till 548, his victory had rendered the Vandals harmless there. Almost exactly a year after setting out from Constantinople, Belisarius was able to reenter the Byzantine capital in triumph with Gelimer, King of the Vandals, an abject prisoner at his side.

In a confident mood Belisarius set out for Italy in 535 to take command of the army which was to overthrow the Ostrogoths. There too all went well for him to begin with. He succeeded in quickly winning back Sicily and Dalmatia and in advancing, if rather more slowly, in southern Italy. Naples and some towns to its south stood out for a while before capitulating and were punished for having done so. Then Belisarius turned on Rome. He attacked the town so unexpectedly and in so spirited a manner that the startled garrison surrendered, opening the town gates to him. Almost as quickly the situation altered, and Belisarius suddenly discovered that he and his men were themselves being besieged within Rome. Quick to appreciate the danger, the Byzantines fought back with great determination and at last managed to break out of the town. The spirit of the men remained high, and undaunted by this setback, Belisarius led them northward to beseige Ravenna, the town which the Ostrogoths had made their capital. In 540, five years after the start of the war, Ravenna, together with the Ostrogoth King Vetiges, surrendered to Belisarius. Belisarius dealt harshly with the inhabitants for having defied him. Then he returned to Constantinople, once again making a triumphal entry to the capital with a defeated king heading his procession of war trophies.

This time Belisarius had misjudged the situation. News quickly reached Constantinople that the Ostrogoths had taken advantage of his absence to rise against the small garrison which he had left in Italy to guard his conquests. Meeting with success, the Ostrogoths formed themselves into an army and set themselves to win back Italy. They were showing themselves capable of doing so.

Although the Ostrogoth victories were not in themselves very important, they seemed so because they were taking place at the very time when the truce purchased from

Persia was due to end. When Justinian tried to obtain an extension, King Chosroes refused to give one. The Persian King thought that the situation gave him a good chance to defeat the Byzantines and he made use of Belisarius' difficulties in Italy to invade Byzantium. After easily overrunning Armenia and Syria, he captured Antioch. Pausing there only long enough to allow his troops to pillage that rich and ancient town, he headed for the Sea of Marmora and met with so little resistance that he soon reached the coast. He was able to gaze across the sea to the opposite shore, where Constantinople lay spread out before him. Justinian hurried to buy another five-year truce from the enemy encamped on his doorstep, and having done so, he once again concentrated his efforts on fighting the Ostrogoths in Italy. However, Belisarius' luck had deserted him. He met with so many reverses that Justinian appointed Narses to succeed him as commander in chief, and although Narses quickly gained control of the situation, it took him till 555 to complete the conquest of Italy. After twenty years of hard and continuous fighting Justinian's dream of a united empire came true. He felt so contented that, in 562, when the Persians again attacked Byzantium, he had no wish to fight back. He settled for a fifty-year peace in return for the annual payment of a handsome sum of money. He failed to notice that Persia's influence was becoming stronger than his own on his eastern borders.

Cultural developments   The long war in Italy had not affected life in Constantinople, where the changes that were taking place in the art and thought of the region, largely brought about by Justinian, were rapidly creating a new Byzantine culture. It was these changes, rather than his success in uniting the empire, which were to make Justinian famous, yet had it not been for his wife, the brave and beautiful Theodora, it is very unlikely that Justinian would have been able to transform Byzantium's early Christian art and culture into a wholly Byzantine idiom.

By Justinian's day Constantinople had naturally altered considerably from what it had been during the reign of Constantine the Great. It had by then grown from the small town laid out by Constantine into a very large one. Indeed, it had outgrown its original boundaries so quickly that

The land walls which Theodosius II built to protect Constantinople

Theodosius II had been obliged to provide it with more space. He had done so by enclosing more land within another magnificent belt of defensive walls, and these walls were to protect the city for almost 1,000 years; they still survive in places, hardly seriously ruined. The population of Constantinople was soon to become larger than that of Rome. The town had acquired a large and busy commercial district, one where craftsmen lived and worked according to their trades, where shops displayed rare and exquisite objects, some made by Byzantium's skillful craftsmen, others imported; most of the latter were luxuries from India and other mysterious Eastern countries, as well as from other parts of the empire, notably Alexandria. The Golden Horn was one of the world's greatest ports and was always thronged with shipping. Many merchants were extremely wealthy and influential, but the landowning aristocracy was even more so. Greeks were coming to the fore and beginning to replace men of Latin origin. They were starting to play an increasingly prominent part at court and in the Senate and the administration.

Unfortunately, the number of poor in Constantinople had also multiplied, and their condition had not improved. Many were indeed so poor that they had little to hope for and little to fear. Whenever they felt that their life had become wholly 31

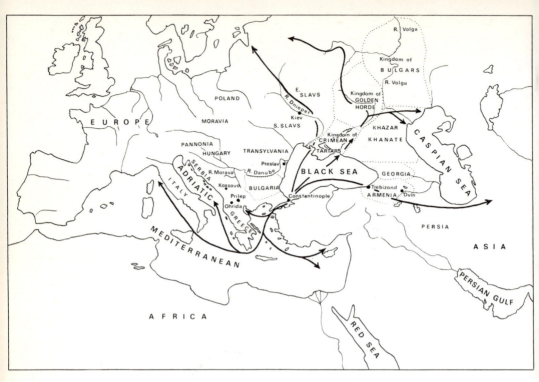

Map indicating Byzantium's major trade routes

unbearable, when bread, which was a government monopoly, rose steeply in price or taxes were increased, they did not hesitate to express their discontent by rioting. Often their risings developed into rebellions, the angry crowds insisting on a change of emperor. A deposed ruler who escaped with his life was indeed fortunate; even one who suffered mutilation, but who was allowed to end his days in a monastery, instead of a prison cell, was considered lucky.

The demes The inhabitants of most large towns were divided into groups or factions called *demes*. At first each town had had four *demes;* each was distinguished by a color which its members displayed on their shoulders by means of a small patch. The four *demes*, were known as the Whites, Reds, Blues, and Greens, but by Justinian's day they had merged into the Blues and Greens. These played much the same part in Byzantine life as do both leading sports teams and political parties in ours, but in addition to filling a sporting and a
32 political role, the members of the *demes* had to undertake

certain public duties. Their leaders were therefore appointed by the government. The *demes* acted as a sort of police force and made sure that their town's walls were kept in good repair and in fit condition to withstand an enemy attack. In times of national emergency they were entitled to arm their supporters. In Constantinople the *demes* also carried out certain duties in the imperial palace and had additional tasks to perform on ceremonial occasions, such as lining the route taken by a procession. It was, however, in the hippodrome that they played their most important role, especially when race meetings or special athletic displays such as the Gothic Games were held there.

The hippodrome served several uses in Byzantium. As its name implies, its purpose was that of a racecourse for charioteers, but like the Forum in Rome, the Agora in Athens, or Speakers Corner in present-day London, it was also used by the public for political meetings. In Constantinople the hippodrome also served as a sort of theater: acrobats, dancers, singers, jugglers, animal trainers and the like performed there either in the intervals between the chariot races or in theatrical performances staged as entertainments for visiting royalty or ambassadors. No Byzantine illustrations of these productions survive, but some do in Russia, for in the eleventh century a Grand Duke of Kiev had the walls of the tower staircase leading from his palace to his private pew in Kiev's Cathedral of Hagia Sophia decorated with paintings illustrating these amusements.

The hippodrome

The games and chariot races organized in Constantinople's hippodrome were state occasions, and the emperor was expected to attend them. It was his duty to give the signal for the start of the first race. Meetings such as these had originally been associated with certain pagan festivities, but they had become so important to the people that the Church had not thought it wise to abolish them. Instead, it had slightly altered their character and timing. The *demes* provided the charioteers, while other members acted as cheerleaders whose job it was to drum up support among the public for their teams. The atmosphere at a race must have been very much the same as that at one of our present-day international football matches, with feelings running even higher in Byzantine Constantinople since the competitors

C

Justinian and Theodora as they appear on the glass mosaic panels
decorating the Church of San Vitale, Ravenna, c 525

represented not only their team and their *deme*, but also a political party. When the inhabitants of Constantinople rioted, one or both *demes* often sided with them, and at times even the athletes did so. When this occurred, the mob often succeeded in setting fire to some important buildings or in smashing the statue of a hated emperor.

Justinian clashed with the Greens when he was still acting *Theodora* as assistant to his uncle, Emperor Justin. This quarrel had led him to favor the Blues, whom he in any case preferred because they shared his views on politics and religion. He had, however, not actively opposed the Greens, for at the time he had other things to think about. Although he was in his late thirties, he had recently fallen in love with an actress of humble birth, but of astonishing beauty and fascination. She was called Theodora and is thought to have been a daughter of a man called Arcadius, a bear keeper in the hippodrome's circus. As a very young child Theodora appeared regularly in the hippodrome's arena as a dancer. When slightly older, she toured North Africa and Asia Minor and also performed in Alexandria. All who saw her were enchanted by her beauty, charm, and grace. Though small, she was very well proportioned; her features were exquisite; her eyes were compelling, her pale complexion was strangely moving. She was about twenty when she returned to Constantinople and Justinian met her and fell hopelessly in love with her. By law Senators were forbidden to marry actresses, but Justinian was so determined to marry Theodora that Justin gave in to him, and in 523 he abolished the law which stood in the way of their marriage. Their wedding took place soon after. Four years later Justinian succeeded to the throne, and Theodora automatically found herself raised to the rank of empress. Although her earlier years had not prepared her for her new duties, in 532 she was to show that she was by instinct well fitted for her position.

On becoming emperor, Justinian began to plan the war in *Riots* North Africa and the later one in Italy. In 531 he imposed much heavier taxes on his people in order to raise funds for the purpose of enlarging and equipping his armies. Although the working classes received the news with anger, the emperor chose that moment to introduce new regulations designed to deprive the *demes* of many of their powers and privileges; he had begun to tire of their insolent airs and quarrelsome behavior. His measures aroused the fury of both *demes*.

Their anger and the people's discontent reached the breaking point in January, 532. A riot broke out in Constantinople, but it was at first no worse a one than many which had occurred in the past, and the authorities were not alarmed by it. At Justinian's orders some of the troublemakers were arrested and brought to trial. Seven were found guilty of murder, a crime punishable by death. Three of them were accordingly sentenced to die by hanging. Two of the condemned belonged to the Green *deme*, the third to the Blue. Executions took place in public in those days, and as was usual, a large crowd gathered to watch the three men die. The hangman must have been either unskilled or somehow personally involved in the event, for he was so clumsy that twice he let the three men drop from the noose alive. As he made ready for a third attempt, some monks in the crowd could no longer endure the horrible sight. Breaking through the mass of spectators, they seized the three condemned men and escaped with them to the Golden Horn. Jumping into a boat, they made off, rowing as fast as they could to the sanctuary offered by the Monastery of St. Laurentius. While the governor of Constantinople was issuing orders to the troops to surround the monastery, both *demes* rushed to the palace to petition Justinian to reprieve the men whom God had spared. Justinian would neither grant them an audience nor even reply to their petition.

Chariot races – a three-day meeting forming part of the annual Christmas festivities – were due to take place in the hippodrome. They were held as usual, and nothing unexpected occurred till late on the last day, when the great crowd of spectators suddenly started shouting, "Long life to the Greens and Blues!" The words indicated that both *demes* were united on the fate of the escaped prisoners. When the last race had been run, it was the *demes* who set up the cry of *"Nika, Nika!"* meaning "Victory, victory!" The words were the signal for the start of the worst revolt in Byzantine history; it came to be known as the Nika Riot. The angry crowd responded to the signal by making for the prisons where they killed the jailers, released the prisoners, and set fire to the buildings. A strong wind was blowing, and by nightfall much of Constantinople was ablaze. The flames raged for several days and ruined the greater part of the imperial palace and many notable government and private buildings, but the destruction of Constantine the Great's Cathedral of Hagia Sophia was the greatest loss of all, for it had come to rank as the Mother Church of Orthodoxy.

The crowd had started by demanding the dismissal of all the officials involved in the sentences passed over the three escaped prisoners and those concerned in carrying them out. Although Justinian had at first ignored these wishes, he was now only too willing to grant them, for the disturbances had taken a very ugly turn. However, he found that the time for doing so had passed; the mob could no longer be controlled. It had grown in size, for many country-men, who had originally come to Constantinople for the Christmas celebrations and who had stayed on for the races, had joined it in order to obtain a reduction in taxation. Feeling that they had got the upper hand, the rioters began to clamor for the removal of Justinian from the throne, instead of merely the dismissal of some of his officials. At this point Constantinople's craftsmen and traders led a nephew of Emperor Anastasius I to the hippodrome and proclaimed him emperor. Justinian was now faced with a revolution.

After a week of street fighting between those loyal to him and the revolutionaries, Justinian felt that he would have to give in. He began to consider ways of escaping from the palace and of finding safety elsewhere. When Theodora learned of this, she hurried to Justinian. She found him consulting with some of his courtiers. Apologizing for her intrusion and for daring to speak her mind before men, she begged Justinian to reconsider his position. Stressing that no man can escape death, she said that she believed exile to be intolerable to a sovereign. "May I never live without this purple robe," she cried, "and may I never live to see the day on which I am no longer addressed as empress by those I meet! If you want to save your life, O Emperor, there is nothing to prevent you from doing so, for we have ample funds, there is the sea, and there are our ships, but consider 37

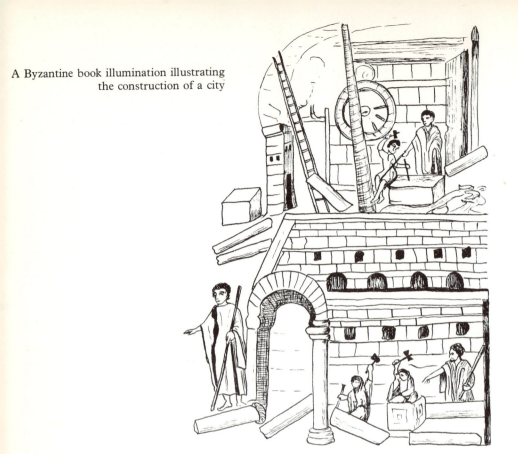

A Byzantine book illumination illustrating
the construction of a city

first whether, on finding yourself in a safe place, you may not prefer death to security. For myself, I agree with the old proverb which says that the imperial purple makes a fine winding sheet, and I desire no better one." Her spirited words heartened Justinian. Two staunch officers – none other than Belisarius and Narses – placed themselves at the head of the loyal troops and engaged the revolutionaries. They strongly resisted them, and the fighting became so bitter that many streets were choked with the dead. More buildings were destroyed, but Justinian gained the upper hand and retained his throne till his death in 565.

Justinian as a patron of art   The Nika Riot made a lasting impression on Justinian. He had always loved scholarship and the arts, finding personal pleasure and contentment in them, but he had probably not appreciated their importance for others. After the Nika rising he actively contributed to their development,

38

devoting as much time to them as he could spare from state affairs and the conduct of wars. The destruction of Hagia Sophia saddened Justinian more than that of any of the other buildings. His decision to replace it by a cathedral of even finer appearance had a far-reaching effect, for it led to the development of a new and adventurous type of church building.

Justinian's artistic taste was as sound as his ability to judge men's characters. He also knew how to bring out the best in artists. When selecting the architects who were to build his new cathedral, he took particular care to find men who would be able to understand and carry out his ideas. He chose two distinguished mathematicians for the purpose one of whom, Anthemius, came from Tralles, and the other, Isidorus, from Miletus.

At the time church architecture had no essentially *The first churche* Christian characteristics. The first Christians had worshiped in secret wherever possible, often using private houses for the purpose. When they were allowed to practice their religion freely, they began by adapting pagan temples to their needs. The churches which they built for themselves a little later were either of the same rectangular shape and flat-roofed form as the temples or circular buildings of the Roman style roofed with a dome. The dome seemed from the start particularly well suited to Christianity because its shape symbolized the sky's; the sky had a special meaning for the early Christians, who believed that paradise was situated just above it. They therefore very much wanted to roof their churches with domes, but they found that a circular building was not really convenient as a church largely because it was impossible to feature its sanctuary, though the presence of the altar there made it most desirable to do so. It was far easier to stress the east end of a rectangular building since the interior could be divided into aisles by means of columns or buttresses, and the central aisle could end in an apse which would set off the altar. In early Christian times builders had not discovered the secret of how to build a round dome above a square or a rectangular building, though in the countries to the east, in Persia, Syria, and perhaps also Armenia, architects were finding a way of doing so. They were solving the difficulty by filling in 39

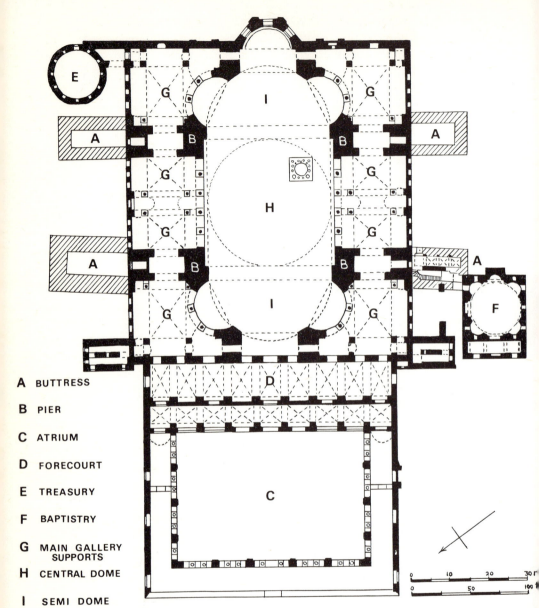

A BUTTRESS

B PIER

C ATRIUM

D FORECOURT

E TREASURY

F BAPTISTRY

G MAIN GALLERY
   SUPPORTS

H CENTRAL DOME

I SEMI DOME

Plan of Justinian's Cathedral of Hagia Sophia, Istanbul

40

the corners of such buildings at roof level in one of two ways, either by building an arch across the corner and so transforming the square into an octagon – this was called a squinch – or by filling it with a triangular structure, its sides curved to fit the base of the dome and the side supports – this one called a pendentive.

Hagia Sophia

Justinian determined to use the latter method for his new cathedral, for it was the more effective as well as the more beautiful. Since the building was to serve as the Mother Church of Orthodoxy, Justinian intended the cathedral to be exceptionally large; he also wanted its dome to be bigger than any other in order that it not only might symbolize heaven, but also give the worshipers assembled under it some idea of what awaited them in paradise. Justinian and his architects minded less about the external appearance of their cathedral than the internal, and it was on the latter that they concentrated their attention. They designed it virtually as a square – it measures some 241 feet long by 244 feet wide – but made it seem more like a rectangle, for its interior is divided into three aisles by magnificent columns. The central aisle was extended to the east end to form a semi-circular apse. They placed the altar in it, erecting a beautifully carved marble screen between it and the nave. A medallion of Christ was placed above the screen's central opening, with one of the Virgin to the right of it and another of St. John to the left, to form what is known as a *deësis* group, and they hung an exquisitely worked silver gauze curtain behind the screen. Until then altars had been very plain, but Justinian arranged for Hagia Sophia's to be richly decorated; by doing so, he set a fashion which was to last for many centuries. A fine late example is the Pala D'Oro in St. Mark's Cathedral in Venice.

The deësis group

The columns which divided the interior of the cathedral into aisles also served to support a wide gallery running along the north, west, and south sides of the building. They were topped with sculptured capitals so deeply undercut that they seem to be made of lace. These uphold graceful arches. The north and south galleries were reserved for women worshipers, who were never admitted to the lower part of a Byzantine church, while the west gallery served for the empress and her ladies. The dome was supported on

The dome

Exterior view of the Cathedral of Hagia Sophia. The minarets were added when, following the conquest of Constantinople by the Ottomans, it was converted into a mosque

four great piers, which terminated the rows of columns separating the aisles. The dome was the wonder of the day because of both its size and its flatness – it seemed like the vault of heaven and appeared to be suspended on invisible chains. It is not its height, therefore, which is so remarkable as its diameter, for its circumference is larger than that of any dome built till a very much later date. Hagia Sophia's dome still ranks as an architectural marvel, and when Sir Christopher Wren was asked to rebuild St. Paul's Cathedral after its destruction in the Great Fire of London, he considered the possibility of roofing it with a dome not unlike Hagia Sophia's. Those who came to worship under Hagia Sophia's dome came almost to believe that they were in heaven's forecourt. The magnificent new cathedral served as a model for other architects for centuries to come, yet it has never been equalled.

The uniqueness of his dome did not satisfy Justinian. He was determined to make the interior a fitting setting for the
dome's splendor, and he devised the most sumptuous

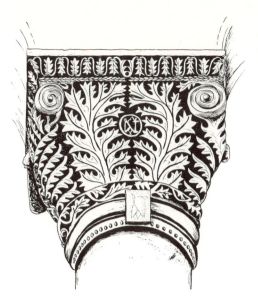

A deeply undercut capital from the
Cathedral of Hagia Sophia with the emperor's
monogram set amidst acanthus leaves

decorations for the purpose. He turned to workers in marble
for the exquisitely veined marble slabs he needed for facing
the lower part of the cathedral's inner walls, as well as for
the geometric marble mosaic compositions which were to
form its floors. Above all, however, he looked to the glass
mosaicists, the artists who created pictures no less beautiful
than the painted ones from tiny gold and many colored
glass cubes. The walls above the marble panels, the sides and
lower sections of the arches, and above all, the apses, the
triangular sections supporting the dome, and the center of
the dome itself were covered with these mosaic compositions. Those in the most important places – that is to say, in
the dome and apses – probably portrayed Christ and the
Virgin; the flat surfaces presented scenes from the Bible,
and later, imperial portraits were added, and here and there
an archangel, an Apostle or Evangelist, while the less important surfaces were covered with most enchanting floral or
geometric compositions. These wonderful decorations were
later added to, altered, and repaired, and on one occasion
they were even destroyed, but the small number of frag-
ments which survive are sufficient to give some idea of the
cathedral's earlier splendor. Although most of the mosaics 43

to be seen today are of later date than Justinian's age, many of them are so fine that they rank with the greatest masterpieces of Christian art.

Craftsmen's guilds   Justinian needed precious vessels, gorgeous vestments, and furnishings for his cathedral. He turned to his finest metalworkers, weavers, and embroiderers for them. These craftsmen belonged to special guilds employed in supplying the emperor and his family, the Church, and certain notables with luxury wares. Any surplus goods belonged to the emperor and could not be sold but were set aside to be used as imperial presents for those kings whom the Byzantine ruler wanted either to honor or to obtain as allies.

The Byzantine guild system dated back to Roman times. By the ninth century as many as twenty-three guilds were registered in Constantinople alone. Their members were governed by very strict rules. No one could belong to more than one guild, but in contrast with ancient Rome, no one was obliged to belong to any. Nor was admission to a guild automatic. An applicant had first to satisfy the guild that he was skilled in his craft and able to pay the guild an entrance fee. Although it was usual for a son to follow in his father's trade, his doing so did not in itself entitle him to membership in his father's guild. Each guild settled the wages which its members were to receive, their conditions of work, and the prices at which their wares could be sold. Wages were paid partly in kind and partly in money. A small breach of regulations was punishable by a fine, more serious cases by expulsion, and some even by mutilation, but a man who had been obliged to resign from a guild was entitled to earn his living by continuing to practice his trade; he had, however, to find employment for himself.

Imperial guilds   Byzantium's most highly prized luxuries came from the East. Silk was at first obtainable only from China; ivory, gems, and spices from India. The best of the locally made luxuries were classed as state monopolies and were made by craftsmen belonging to the imperial guilds. These ranked above the ordinary guilds, and their workshops were situated in the grounds of the imperial palace. The Guild of the Purple Dyers was the oldest of these. It produced all the purple-colored materials used by the emperor and his family. The Imperial Guild of Metalworkers made all the

(*Right*) This magnificent fifth century silver-gilt amphora from Concesti was made for secular use and is therefore decorated with scenes of classical character
(*Left*) A fine fifth century silver vessel of Syrian workmanship found at Homs. It is adorned with medallions containing the busts of Christ and the apostles

gold and silver objects needed by the emperor. Silver was so scarce in early Byzantine times that it was more expensive than gold. Most of the supply was reserved for the emperor, and the little that was sold to others was heavily taxed. The silver objects made in the imperial workshops were stamped either with the emperor's monogram, that of the governor of Constantinople, or that of the controller of the mint, much as silver is hallmarked in Britain today. These objects made splendid imperial gifts for the barbarian chieftains whom the emperors were anxious to appease. Many of the tiny, exquisite gold cloisonné enamels which the Byzantines used to decorate the most precious of their gold and silver caskets, church vessels, Gospel covers, crosses, and jewelry were made in this workshop. The highest technical skill was needed to produce them. Together with the miniature glass mosaic pictures, where each cube is the size of a pinhead, they rank with the most delicate products of the jeweler's craft.

Of all the luxuries known to the ancient world, silk was the most highly valued and the most sought after, and for that very reason Cleopatra refused to wear anything else. The Chinese had discovered how to make silk as far back as

The silk trade

45

the ninth century BC, but they treated the knowledge as the most important of their state secrets. For centuries the export of silk was forbidden by the Emperor of China, and the first pieces to reach Europe had probably been smuggled out of the country. However, in the second century BC the Emperor Wu-ti decided to export a very small amount of silk in return for certain Western specialties, especially glass and lucerne. The amount fell far short of the West's demand, for the supply was closely regulated; no European merchants were allowed ever to enter China in order to buy the silk direct or to collect the bales. Instead, the bales were loaded onto Chinese caravans and carried to what is now Afghanistan, where they were unloaded and then reloaded onto foreign caravans to travel westward along the Great Silk Road. In 106 BC the first through caravan delivered the bales as far as Persia, but the amount of silk remained very small. The Byzantines tried to discover new ways of increasing the supply, but they were always unsuccessful. Then, in 552, two missionaries discovered the secret of silk production. They managed to smuggle some silkworms and mulberry leaves out of China in their walking sticks and, on reaching Constantinople, sold them to the emperor. Shortly afterward an imperial silk-weaving workshop was established in the grounds of the imperial palace. The materials produced in it carried the emperor's monogram

This lion – a symbol of majesty – comes from a silk of late tenth/early eleventh century. The elephant appears in the roundels forming the main design of a tenth century silk twill. Both were woven in Constantinople

46

The man shooting backward in the Parthian manner is the chief motif of a superb eleventh century silk woven in Constantinople

woven into their selvages. Their export was forbidden, and their distribution was even more strictly controlled than that of the finest metalwork. Clear regulations laid down exactly who among the emperor's subjects were to be permitted to buy and wear silk. Those court ladies who were entitled to do so were obliged to obtain it from the imperial sale rooms which were situated in the grounds of the palace, in a building called the House of Lamps, because the light was kept burning in it throughout the night.

Justinian was a great reader, and although Latin continued to rank as the official language, the pleasure he found in Greek classics brought about a renewed interest in them. Greek influence is reflected in the secular art of the period, for it became fashionable to decorate the finest silver dishes and similar objects with mythological scenes and other Greek designs. The enchanting marble mosaic pavement which was recently discovered by British archeologists in the grounds of the imperial palace partly shows Greek influence,

Scholarship

47

although the idyllic illustrations of nature and country life are far more Latin in character.

The Monophysites Although Justinian appreciated the beauty of Greek art, he closed Athens' ancient university in 529 because certain subjects taught there were based on pagan philosophy. The emperor was extremely religious. He expressed his faith in hymns of his own composition, some of which remain in use today in the Orthodox Church, and he also wrote essays on religious subjects. Like Constantine the Great, Justinian wished the Church to grow in strength and influence; like Constantine, he continued to preside at its councils and often tried to impose his wishes on it. He did not always succeed in this, but on at least one occasion it would have been better had the Church followed his advice. The matter concerned a group of ardent Eastern Christians calling themselves Monophysites. In early Christian times they had reached a different conclusion from that of the established Church concerning the nature of Christ, believing that God the Father, Son, and Holy Ghost were not a divine trinity, but that each formed part of a single being and that Christ had a single nature, not a dual one. Both the Western and the Eastern branches of the Church had agreed in condemning the Monophysites at the Council of the Churches which met at Chalcedon in 451, and both had joined in proclaiming them heretics. The Monophysites took no notice of these rulings and continued to hold and preach their views so loudly and insistently that the Pope severed all relations with them. When Justinian became emperor, he tried to bring about a reconciliation, but neither the Pope nor the Patriarch of Constantinople would agree to it.

Byzantium's first university Constantine the Great had provided Constantinople with an academy to serve as a center for advanced studies. In 425 Emperor Theodosius II conferred university status on it. Justinian took great interest in it, encouraging both its secular and its religious faculties. Printing was unknown to the Byzantines, and all their books were therefore in manuscript form, each volume being copied by a scribe either from an original work or from an existing version. Books were, as a result, scarce and expensive.

Justinian discovered that the empire's laws were often being incorrectly applied largely because they were not

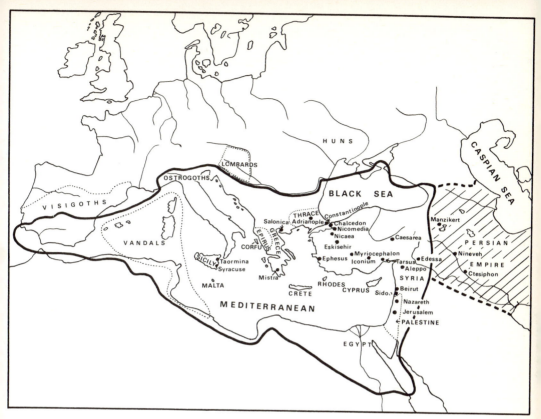

Map of Byzantium when at its largest

available to lawyers in book form and partly because they were outdated. Emperor Theodosius II had already realized that it would be helpful if the laws were collected into a book, and some had been assembled at his orders in a book called the Codex Theodosianus, but many more had not been included in it. Justinian therefore employed a group of lawyers to complete the task by collecting all the laws relating to the country's constitution. After only fourteen months' work they had done as he asked, compiling a book called the Codex Constitutiorum or Justinianus. It proved so useful that in 534 and again in 536, the laws which Justinian had introduced were added to it. Meanwhile, another group of lawyers had been engaged in examining the remaining laws, abolishing those which they considered useless and deciding on the verdicts to be passed in cases where similar crimes had until then often been punished by different sentences. This 49

D

was a more difficult undertaking than the first, but it was accomplished by 533. The new digest contained 9,123 laws based on the rulings reached by thirty-nine lawyers. The book was warmly welcomed, for its existence made it easier for lawyers to apply the law in a similar manner throughout the empire and for individuals to discover exactly what was and what was not legal. It influenced Western Europe's legal system and is still studied by students of law.

Theodora died after some twenty-five years of married life. Justinian outlived her by almost as many more. He was fortunate in never realizing that the empire he had taken such pains to unify would soon fall apart again and that new enemies in the West, such as the Lombards in Italy and the Bulgars and Slavs in the Balkans, would deprive it of many of the territories which had once been part of it. He could, however, have drawn lasting satisfaction from the know-ledge that he had succeeded in making Constantinople lovelier than most other towns, a city where the arts flourished more gloriously than anywhere else, and that he had made Byzantium the embodiment of Christianity, the place where people were more concerned over the salvation of their souls than in acquiring material wealth, where learning, though closely linked to theology, did not wholly neglect secular subjects. The importance which Justinian attached to industry and trade had led to their being state-controlled, but the state also encouraged their development and protected them. On the other hand, Justinian's wars had exhausted the nation, and his taxes had impoverished the people with the result that he was intensely disliked by many of his subjects. Yet his legal reforms had made their lives easier, and his patronage of artists and craftsmen had pro-vided many of them with exhilarating work. The hatred they felt for Justinian has become a thing of the past, as have his military conquests, but the culture which he created survives to glorify Byzantium, for it was largely owing to his efforts that throughout much of its history, Constantinople proved as stimulating an artistic center as Florence in Renaissance Italy and Paris in nineteenth-century Europe.

CHAPTER THREE

The Byzantine Way of Life

CHRISTIANITY and the arts which were largely devoted to glorifying it were subjects of absorbing interest to the Byzantines. Their lives centered on their religion because it promised them the chance of eternal life in the celestial kingdom. For each of them the salvation of his soul was therefore a matter of the gravest importance. It had also been so for the early Christians who had tried to achieve it by martyrdom. When the law permitted the practice of Christianity, the faithful ceased to be tortured, and those who felt more concerned about their future life than their earthly one had been obliged to seek new ways of qualifying for the Almighty's grace. *Devotion to Christianity*

Many thought they might succeed in doing so by withdrawing to the Egyptian desert to live the solitary life of hermits. Those who did so spent their time in prayer and in inflicting pain on their bodies in order to subdue the physical side of their nature to the spiritual. Some gradually acquired a reputation for saintliness and attracted followers, who settled at their sides to live in a similar manner. In some cases the small group of men who were trying to live righteously built a hostel for themselves, and some of these later expanded into monasteries. Although one of the first monasteries was found by St. Anthony, it was the one which St. Basil, Bishop of Caesarea, founded in the fourth century which became the model for most later foundations. Every monastery was controlled by an abbot. Since few of them would allow any but the holiest monks to live alone as hermits, the number of hermits gradually decreased, while that of the monasteries and convents multiplied. To begin with, the men and women who took their vows were not allowed any personal possessions. Even their clothes belonged to the monastery. *Monasticism*

51

Monasticism instantly appealed to the Byzantines. Many took their vows late in life in order to end their days in these God-fearing surroundings; others did so early in life and were therefore never able to marry and have children. At certain periods so many people entered monasteries and convents that the emperors feared that Byzantium would become underpopulated, and they therefore tried to stem the movement. At the same time, however, they attempted to earn forgiveness for their sins by founding monasteries and by showering valuable gifts on those already in existence. As a result, the monks forgot their vows of poverty, and many monasteries acquired great wealth and much land. Many abbots were no longer content to provide their monks with the opportunity of devoting their lives to prayer and fasts; they now encouraged them to use their talents to glorify God and to help their fellowmen.

As a result, many monasteries became great centers of learning, and practically all of them developed into charitable institutions, some serving as hospitals and others as schools. Many possessed workshops where religious paintings were produced, theological books transcribed and often adorned with painted illuminations. The Monastery of St. Catherine on Mount Sinai was one of the first to become an important center of religious thought, learning, and the arts; it is also one of the few which survive with many of its contents more or less intact. The objects collected in its treasury throughout the centuries testify to the veneration in which it has been held by generations of Christians.

The monastic communities of Mount Athos in northern Greece are an even more remarkable survival. Just over 1,000 years ago, in the year 963, a priest called Alexius was a friend of Emperor Nicephorus Phocas. With the emperor's encouragement he withdrew to the small, mountainous promontory situated near Thessalonica which is known to us now as the Holy Mountain and founded the Monastery of the Lavra there. It was the first of many such foundations.

In due course there were 23 religious institutions, ranging in size from the tiny hermitage to the vast monastery poised on the peninsula's precipitous peaks or clinging to its ridges like limpets. At times as many as 8,000 to 10,000 monks lived in them, devoting themselves to a life of prayer

52

The Monastery of Chilandari on Mount Athos founded early in the
fourteenth century

and fasting. The monks dedicated the promontory as a
whole to the Virgin, and in order to honor her, they forbade
all female beings, whether human or animal, ever to set foot
on its soil. The prohibition remains in force there today, one
or two monasteries making an exception in the case of hens
or cats. No woman may therefore visit Mount Athos to gaze
in wonder and respect at the spectacular buildings which
the monks erected for themselves there or to see the religious
paintings with which they adorned the walls of their churches
or the ancient treasures assembled in their treasuries and
libraries in the course of 1,000 years.

At Nicephorus Phocas' orders Mount Athos was granted
the right to govern itself, but in 1312, when times were difficult, Emperor Andronicus II brought it under imperial
jurisdiction in order to protect it. Today it forms a part of
Greece but retains a considerable measure of independence.
Life has stood as still on Mount Athos for 1,000 years as it
did for 100 in the case of the Sleeping Beauty. Although the
number of monks living there today is very small, their way   53

of life has scarcely altered from that laid down by Alexius for the first monks of the Lavra.

In Byzantium laymen were hardly less troubled than monks over the state of their souls. Salvation seemed to them to depend not only on their ability to obey the Christian rule, but also on their ability to interpret it with complete accuracy. This was no easy matter, and their attempts to discover the real meaning of sentences in the Gospel led some of them to come to different conclusions from those reached by the established Church. When that happened, the senior clergy would condemn their doctrine. When they took no notice of such rulings the Church often felt obliged to brand them as freethinkers or heretics. There were many heretical sects in Byzantium. Some were small and unimportant and soon petered out, but several attracted so many followers that they caused the Church serious concern. Two were especially troublesome. One consisted of Arians, followers of a man called Arius, who affirmed that Christ was only part divine. The other was the Monophysite sect. The Church fought all heresies with great determination, lest they lead to a revival of paganism, but it was especially opposed to the larger sects, for these challenged the unity of the Church, a unity which was already weakened by the Church's division into two branches – the Catholic and the Orthodox.

Nevertheless, the established church remained supreme and able to impose its authority on all its members, regardless of their class or occupation. The duties which the Church allotted to the emperor were especially numerous and important since, as Christ's vicar on earth, the emperor acquired some element of divinity. His throne was therefore made the width of a double throne. On Sundays and religious holidays its right half belonged to Christ, and on these days a volume of the Gospel was therefore placed there to make this obvious to all. At such times the emperor occupied the left side of the throne and acted merely in a secular capacity; on all other occasions he sat on the right of the throne, and when he did so, he acted not only as emperor, but also as Christ's vice-regent. Because of his dual role, his palace was generally referred to as the sacred palace, and in art, he was often shown wearing a halo. His position made it necessary for him to officiate in certain religious services, especially those conducted by the Patriarch of Constantinople in the Cathedral of Hagia Sophia at Christmas and at Easter. The patriarch ranked as second in importance to the emperor and therefore lived in great state. He had a palace of his own and also official apartments in Hagia Sophia. He often entertained the emperor in both and was in return entertained by the emperor in the imperial palace.

All Byzantines spent a large part of their day at prayer. *Religion and* They were obliged to go to Church on Sundays, and those *the family* who failed to do so on three successive Sundays ran the risk of excommunication. The Church not only directed their lives, but also played a prominent part in them. It christened each one at birth and later confirmed him. Marriage engagements were considered almost as important as the actual wedding and of similar religious significance. The family's priest therefore took a leading part at an engagement ceremony, and a breach of the engagement was punishable by a fine. Later the family priest married the couple, and it was he who buried them when they died. Secular amusements were rare, and at the Church's insistence, life revolved around the family, where women were as influential as men. Even though women took no part in public life, since it was considered unsuitable for them to appear at official festivities, the importance which the Church attached to family life gave them as much power in the home as their husbands. As a result, women came to be respected, and the *The status of* law made a point of protecting their interests and personal *women* incomes. Nevertheless, it was not considered necessary for women to be well educated. Most men could read and write, and girls were also generally taught to do so, but they advanced beyond that stage only in the richer families. In these, tutors were often engaged to teach the boys, and the girls were generally allowed to share their brothers' lessons. Even in such families the boys were generally sent to school on reaching the age of fourteen. Sometimes, however, they continued to be tutored at home until they entered the university, and their sisters were, as a result, able to carry their studies to an advanced stage, but even the cleverest girls could not enter a university. Those who wanted to pursue their studies further had to do so privately with a 55 tutor. Quite a number did so, and some acquired the reputation of bluestockings.

Education Most education was religious in character, and even secular education was closely linked to theology. Children were expected to know the whole Bible by heart at an early age, but they were not obliged to have memorized Aesop's fables till they were fourteen. At school they were taught grammar and syntax in addition to reading, writing, and arithmetic. They also had to learn fifty lines of Homer a day, and when they knew the whole of the *Odyssey*, they moved on to the *Iliad*. At fourteen boys started to learn the art of public speaking by studying the works of such great prose writers as Demosthenes. In their last year at school they studied the sciences; these consisted of advanced arithmetic, geometry, music, anatomy, and astrology. By the sixth century most children of freemen were being educated free of charge in state-owned schools or in orphanages which had been founded by emperors or prosperous noblemen. By the eleventh century the free schools were open to all children regardless of nationality or class. So, too, from an early date were the religious schools run by many of the monasteries, as well as by each bishopric, for boys intending to enter the Church. There the teachers were monks, and theology formed the main subject. By 1045 Constantinople possessed three universities. Medicine had become so important that it was taught in one of them together with botany and zoology, those qualifying in it working as doctors either in the state-run hospitals or in the army's medical corps. Another of the universities specialized in law.

Naming a child At birth a newly born baby was washed and tightly swaddled or bandaged in strips of woolen material. It was kept wrapped in this way for the first two months of its life. It was christened within eight weeks of its birth. The church at first recognized only the one name given to a child or person on Baptism. A Greek Christian therefore had only one name until the sixth century, when surnames came into use. In order to distinguish him from others of the same name the habit grew up of following it by his father's name in its genitive case – that is to say, by his patronymic. For example, if a child's name was Peter and his father's Nicholas, he 56 was known as Peter, son of Nicholas. If the family was of

A mural panel of the Nativity executed in glass mosaic for Kariye
Djami, Istanbul, c 1320

Roman descent, the Roman system was adopted – it was
made up of his praenomen, first name, or number followed
by his nomen gentilianum, clan name, ending with his
family's name, his cognomen.

Children became engaged when very young, the choice of *Marriage*
partner being decided by their parents, but girls were forbidden by law to marry until they were twelve years old and
boys fourteen. Weddings were celebrated with great
solemnity in church and much gaiety and ceremonial in the
home.

There were no organized public amusements for women *Diversions*
and very few for men, although the latter were able to live a
more varied life than the women. Men could meet at will in
one of the town's many marketplaces to hear the news of the
day or sit in the public gardens or squares, but women could
not do so, even though Constantinople was noted for the
beauty and large number of its public squares and gardens. 57

It was not even considered right for women to go out into the street alone. Since even some humble households possessed either a couple of slaves or a servant who helped their mistress with the housework and bought the food daily at the local market, there was generally someone able to accompany her and her daughters when they needed to go out, but they could do so only in order to go to church, to visit relations, or, if the family was too poor to have a private bathhouse, to go to the public baths. These were open to men throughout the day, but they were reserved for women in the evenings.

Women stayed at home for days on end, spending much of their time doing exquisite embroidery, while their children played at their sides. They had some toys to amuse them, but once again, the boys came off better than the girls. They had model horses, carts, and houses made of clay, earth, or stone, as well as tops, hoops, knucklebones, balls, whistles and flutes, while the girls had wax, clay, or plaster dolls. But childhood ended early in Byzantium, and toys were set aside as children neared their teens.

Apart from family events such as the birth of a child, its engagement and marriage, the withdrawal to a monastery or nunnery of a member of the family, and, to some extent, a funeral, the major events in the lives of women were provided by the Church. The great festivals of Christmas and Easter ranked as the year's highlights, but time was also

A table laid for a meal; note the round loaves with crosses on them

broken up by the fasts prescribed by the Church, by pilgrimages to neighboring shrines or monasteries, or at times by a period of retreat in a convent. Although the Church put a stop to the pagan feasts which had played a very important part in people's lives in earlier times, some continued to rank as holidays till as late as the eighth century. On these occasions young men continued to parade the streets in fancy dress, and the women were able to watch them pass from their windows and balconies. Every month youths welcomed the new moon by lighting huge bonfires in the streets and leaping over the flames. The gruesome sight of a prisoner being led to death or torture seated back to front on a donkey with his hands tied behind his back and his head shaved also attracted much attention, men rushing to follow him in order to see the sentence carried out. Sometimes there was an ambassadorial procession to watch. Always a sight of great magnificence, it could also be exciting, for embassies from Eastern countries often included extraordinary animals such as elephants and giraffes in their processions. Men could also look forward to the great annual fairs, where traveling actors, acrobats, and animal trainers could always be seen. The visits of astrologers and fortune-tellers were popular, for the genuine belief of the Byzantines in the Christian religion did not prevent them from being exceedingly superstitious. Even as late as the eleventh century Emperor Alexius Comnenus was in the habit of regularly consulting his court astrologer, and he was in no way exceptional in this. Professional storytellers made a point of visiting householders, and an entire household would collect to listen to their lively recitations.

It was from the race meetings and games held regularly in the hippodrome that the men derived their keenest pleasure and excitement. Though pagan in origin, these entertainments were so popular that they were retained in Christian times, continuing to play a very important part in the lives of townsmen, each of whom was entitled to attend them free of charge, on presentation of a token. Constantinople's hippodrome was enclosed by tiers of marble benches capable of seating an audience of 40,000 men. It was long and rounded at one end. A row of monuments set in a straight line along its center divided the track into an upward

The hippodrome games

59

and a downward course. Three of the monuments are still standing in their original positions in Istanbul, in what is now a public garden. One, an obelisk which Emperor Theodosius I brought from Egypt for the purpose, is set on a base decorated with sculptures showing him attending one of the hippodrome's race meetings; another is a column formed of three intertwined bronze serpents – it was brought to Byzantium from Delphi and had the names of all the states that took part in the Battle of Plataea engraved on it. The third was also an obelisk, originally coated in bronze, set up by Emperor Constantine Porphyrogenitus. Each side of the course was wide enough for four chariots to race abreast. Each chariot was drawn by four horses and was therefore called a quadriga. The charioteers had to be extremely skillful if accidents were to be avoided. They raced in short-sleeved tunics pulled in at the waists by a leather belt held firm by shoulder bands. They protected their legs with leather leggings. The charioteers were members of the demes and displayed their colors on their shoulders. They were as much admired as are present-day athletes. Each had his own supporters, and some emperors even had statues made of their favorite drivers.

The emperor was greatly involved in the hippodrome's sporting events. His permission to hold a race meeting had to be applied for two days in advance. The day after notices announcing the event were posted on the entrances to the hippodrome, and the two demes met at the gate which connected the grounds of the imperial palace to the hippodrome. They started by cheering the emperor and wishing their own deme success in the coming contest. Then they moved on to inspect the stables and the horses chosen to run in the races. These were situated close to a gate opening directly onto the course. They were admirably kept and very splendid. The gold harness belonging to each horse hung above the entrance to its stall. The demes carefully examined each animal to make sure that it was well and fit to race.

On the day of the races the hippodrome's gates were opened at dawn to admit the public. On rising, the emperor put on his robes of state. Wearing his full regalia and carrying a lighted candle, he went, as he always did, to pray in his private chapel. The master of the horse was by then busily making sure that the charioteers were in their places, that the leaders of the demes had not forgotten to bring their standards, that their members were ready to carry out the duties allotted to them, and that the hippodrome's seats were filled. The emperor had probably by that time reached the audience chamber adjoining the hippodrome's imperial box and begun to greet the notables whom he had invited to watch the races with him. When the master of the horse entered the hall and informed the emperor that everything was ready, the doors to the imperial box would slowly open. The emperor would pass through them to enter his box and mount the steps leading to his throne. Standing in front of it, he would face the audience. Raising a fold of his robe, he would proceed to bless the people in the seats opposite him by making the sign of the cross with it; then he would turn to his right and bless the people there, then to his left. Having

This sculpture still stands in the hippodrome at Istanbul. It shows the Emperor Theodosius in his box with his courtiers and guardsmen on either side of him. Below members of the factions holding organs with dancers and entertainers standing by

done so, he would raise a white handkerchief, giving the signal for the first race to start by letting it fall. As he did so, the stable doors would fly open, and the first four chariots would race onto the track.

Eight races were run daily, the meetings generally lasting for three days. The charioteers had drawn their positions by lot. They had to complete seven rounds of the course in each race. The count was kept by means of a vast stand which could be seen clearly by all. Seven ostrich eggs were set up on it, one of which was removed as the last chariot completed a circuit. The governor of Constantinople, wearing a toga, presented the winners of individual races with a crown or palm at the end of each day, but on the last day the final prize was presented to the winning team by the emperor; it generally consisted of a golden emblem, a silver ornament, and a belt.

After the fourth race of the day, at half time, there was an interval for refreshments, when the emperor entertained his guests to luncheon. During the shorter intervals between each race mimes, acrobats, actors, dancers, animal trainers, and jugglers rushed onto the course in much the same way as clowns do in a present-day circus and proceeded to entertain the audience. The dances were generally performed by children. They sometimes also appeared in the theatrical entertainments produced by adults in the hippodrome to amuse foreigners paying a state visit to Constantinople, but these productions were less popular among Constantinopolitans than the individual turns performed by acrobats, singers and jugglers.

Housing   Throughout Byzantium the poor – and the towns swarmed with them – lived in hovels. From the fifth century on Constantinople's authorities tried to solve the slum problem by building skyscraper tenements – buildings anything from five to nine stories high. They divided them into flatlets, which they let to workmen and artisans, but even in these the overcrowding and poverty soon became so great that the blocks were even more vile to live in than the wretched single-story shanties in which most of the poor lived. People with even quite a small income, on the other hand, were well housed, and the rich lived in splendid mansions.

This ruined mansion in Istanbul is one of the very few examples of domestic architecture to survive. It is known as Justinian's House

The first houses to be built in Constantinople were generally two stories high and had no windows facing the street; for security reasons, they gave onto courtyards around which the houses were built, as did the stables, cattle sheds, kennels, storerooms, and so on. These courts were generally large enough for the owners to exercise their horses in. The family's well was also situated there, and very wealthy people built their bathhouses either in their courtyards or in their gardens. By the fifth century higher houses were being built; these were given windows facing onto the street, though still not at sidewalk level. When it became usual for houses to have windows overlooking the street, a law was passed obliging streets to be at least 12 feet wide; when balconies became popular, they had by law to be at least 15 feet above street level, nor was one house allowed to spoil another's view of the sea, an ancient monument, or a fine statue. Windows were made of small square or rectangular panes of glass fitted into stucco panels, for the Byzantines were unable to make large panes of glass, and even the small 63

Tables such as these could be used as desks or writing tables

ones were very expensive. Many windows were provided with decorative iron railings. For similar security reasons, many front doors were also made of iron; others were made of thick and strong wood studded with iron nails.

The rooms inside these houses were built around a large central hall of roof height. In private houses the men often used it as a reception room, while businessmen used it for the display and sale of goods. The halls were bordered with columns, which supported a gallery and provided entry to the storerooms and domestic offices that occupied the rest of the ground floor. The family's living rooms were situated on the first floor and were entered from the gallery; the bedrooms and the living rooms used by the women and children were above them, for although women were not segregated as in a Moslem country, they nevertheless lived a retired life, spending most of their time in their own quarters. Many of the richer houses also had a private chapel in their grounds.

Furniture   Houses such as these were very comfortable to live in. Since the winters can be very cold in Constantinople and Asia Minor, the Roman hypocaust system of central heating was installed in many of them, while others were heated with charcoal braziers. They were well furnished. Beds had either square or turned legs and plain head pieces; tables were round, square, T- or D-shaped. The emperor and 64 certain of his courtiers owned large dining tables made of ivory inlaid with gold. In early times the Byzantines had taken their meals reclining on couches in the Roman manner, a practice which was followed at court on ceremonial occasions even in the tenth century, although well before that date it had become usual to eat sitting up at a table. They used benches, stools, and chairs for the purpose. Most chairs resembled Roman ones, for they continued to be mounted on lion-shaped feet and to have their sides and backs decorated with winged victories, dolphins, and lyres. Folding stools were also used, as well as low, built-in cupboards which seldom contained more than one shelf, lecterns, and desks shaped rather like a Victorian davenport. Clothes and household linen were kept in chests, for the Byzantines knew nothing about chests of drawers or tall, hanging cupboards.

Cooking was done on charcoal. Food of many kinds was *Meals* easy to obtain, and meals were varied, elaborate, carefully cooked, and often accompanied by complicated sauces. Tables were well laid, the cloths often being beautifully embroidered; napkins were provided from an early date, and spoons, knives, and even forks were in general use. Forks may have been invented in the East, rather than in Byzantium, but they were so widely used there that a Byzantine princess who married a doge of Venice took some with her to her new home. The Venetians had never seen forks until she did so and began by thinking them comic, but they quickly started using them, too, and it was probably they who introduced them to Western Europe. The Byzantines were in the habit of eating three meals a day with fruit and vegetables forming an important part of their diet. They ate goat's meat, as well as mutton, and much poultry and game, as well as fish. Constantinopolitans were obliged by law to keep three months' food supply in their storerooms for use if their city were besieged.

The Byzantines were so fond of good drinking water that *Water* they could grade its quality in the same way as we do that of wine. They also appreciated its importance in the house. Their supply had to be brought to them by a series of aqueducts, one of which, that of Emperor Valens, still survives as a splendid ruin in the heart of old Istanbul. They quickly realized how easy it would be for an enemy to cut off their 65

E

The Cistern of 1001 Columns,
Istanbul

supply and, by depriving them of water, oblige them to
surrender. They therefore built themselves a series of underground cisterns capable of storing vast quantities of water.
The finest are so large and so well built and their roofs are
supported by such splendid columns and capitals that they
are as impressive as a church. One of the most remarkable
of these cisterns is situated near Hagia Sophia. The Turks
aptly named it the Underground Palace. Another they
called the Cistern of a Thousand and One Columns, for like
the trees in a wood, there seem to be more of them than
can be counted.

Life in the country was pleasant for the rich and difficult
for the peasants, most of whom were very poor. Their imple-

ments were primitive, consisting of very simply constructed wooden plows pulled by oxen or mules, a double-pointed hoe, a two-pronged fork, spades, mattocks, double-headed mallets, planting sticks consisting of a pointed stone prod fixed to a wooden handle, and so on. Many peasants, whether freemen or slaves, were employed by monasteries, others by wealthy landowners, and only a very few were self-employed smallholders. The lives of all were equally hard, for they had to work long hours and to pay very heavy taxes. Rebellions and riots were not uncommon among them. Their pleasures were few and similar to those of countrymen the world over; they consisted of hunting expeditions, quiet hours spent fishing, harvest suppers, meetings with neighbors at locally held markets and fairs, and above all, religious festivals and family celebrations.

In the seventh century a new sort of person settled in the areas bordering Byzantium's eastern frontiers. At the time the army was very short of men, and soldiers were desperately needed on all frontiers, particularly in the east, where the Arabs had become aggressive neighbors. Emperor Heraclius tried to overcome the shortage by attracting volunteers for service in the East by promising each recruit

Theme holdings

Ornamental wells of a type found in the grounds of private houses

67

An ivory of a blacksmith and his wife working their forge; they represent Adam and Eve

a strip of agricultural land known as a theme. A theme holder could think of his plot as his own during his lifetime. He could live on it with his wife and children and cultivate it for his own advantage, but in return he had to promise to carry out certain military duties. These included acting as a sort of passport control officer by examining the documents belonging to people traveling in his district. He had also to perform sentry duty on one of the many turrets which had been built along the border. These towers were placed between 3,000 and 4,000 feet apart and were so situated that each sentry could see the turret on either side; he could warn neighboring sentries by means of signals, if he saw an enemy approaching. If war broke out, the theme holder was obliged to report to a rallying point fully armed and mounted. At his death one of his sons could take over the theme on the same conditions as those on which his father had held it, but the others had to leave home on reaching manhood. They were encouraged to settle as freemen on a piece of abandoned, though fertile, land and to work it as a small holding for their own advantage since, by doing so, they contributed to the country's food supplies.

Until the sixth century many Byzantines had worn the Roman toga, and there was nothing in their costume to distinguish a layman from a priest. When the toga started to go out of fashion, the priests replaced it by a long, fairly tight-fitting robe buttoning down the front, very like those in use in Orthodox countries today. They also started wearing vestments when officiating in church. Court officials were provided with their robes of office; these differed in color and trimmings according to the wearer's rank and occupation and to that extent were not unlike a uniform. On Easter Sunday each of them received a new tunic and belt from the emperor's hands at a special investiture held in the imperial palace.

Fashions in clothes changed very slowly in Byzantium, yet the appearance of civilians altered considerably over the years. Among the women the hairstyles changed more often than those of their clothes. At times they parted their hair in the center and coiled it at the sides; at other times they piled it high on their heads. Sometimes they wore gold circlets or tortoiseshell combs, and almost always those who could afford to do so strung gold, silver, or pearl chains

This tiger hunt comes from a sixth century marble floor mosaic in the Great Palace, Constantinople

Gold cloisonné enamel plaques of two saints and two dancing girls, all wearing elegant tunics and skirts. From an eleventh century crown

through their hair. They were also in the habit of making up their faces very heavily. Theodora and the later empresses, as well as their court ladies, adapted the emperor's state robe to their own need. Their costume consisted of a long silk tunic or caftan worn under a long, straight garment called a dalmatic; the latter was trimmed with embroidery, sometimes with jewels, around the neck, shoulders, and hem. Over it they placed a long piece of thin, exquisitely embroidered material which had a hole cut at its center so that they could put their heads through it; it had a long panel at the back which either could become a train or, women's hats being unknown, could be drawn over the head like a scarf with the end draped over the left arm.

Poorer women also wore variants of their husbands' clothes. These consisted of an open tunic worn over an undergarment having a side panel of sufficient length to form a head scarf. Although in later times some owned a best dress made of silk, the majority made their dresses of wool, linen, or a very fine and cool cotton. Since the cotton was transparent, the Church tried to prevent women wearing it on the grounds of unseemliness, but many nevertheless continued to make it up into dresses. They generally trimmed their clothes with the beautiful embroidery they were so skillful at producing. In cold weather all women wore cloaks like the one in which Empress Theodora appears in the mosaic portrait made in her lifetime in Ravenna. In the eleventh century top garments were cut on princess lines; the tunics had close-fitting bodices and were tightly waisted, the lower section being either flared or cut on the round. Necklines varied, some being square, others round, boat, or V-shaped. Shoes had no heels. Women liked dressing in white or pastel shades, as well as in glowing colored brocades. They had a greater understanding of personal cleanliness than was to be found in Europe even as late as the eighteenth century, for they made a point of frequently changing their clothes in order that they might be washed or cleaned, and even the poor went to the public baths at least once a week. These were equipped with private cubicles, lavatories, and basins, as well as with hot and cold pools and halls. Wealthy women bathed frequently in their private bathhouses.

The Byzantines loved finely worked jewelry. Here are examples of bracelets

Men were more fashion-conscious than women, perhaps because of their freer and fuller lives. In the seventh century they became very interested in the Eastern world. As a result, they gave up wearing sandals of the Roman type, replacing them in summer by shoes of Eastern shape and in winter by soft leather boots. At the same time they stopped wearing the short, loose tunics which their fathers had substituted for the toga and appeared in short, tight-fitting tunics which had to have a triangular-shaped piece of material inserted in the center of the back to allow for freedom of movement. These tunics were finished off with small collars. Clothes inspired by Syrian, Bulgarian, and Italian styles were fashionable at one time or another, and at a late date so were the Turkish. The early Byzantines had been clean-shaven and had worn their hair short like the Romans, but in Justinian's day mustaches and beards came into fashion, and although hair was kept short in front and at the sides, it was allowed to grow long at the back. By the seventh century dandies were plaiting or curling their waist-long tresses. By the eighth century public opinion was so opposed to a hairy man that a law was passed forcing men to shave. When Theophilus, who was bald, came to the throne, he obliged

Two rings chosen from a wide variety

Byzantine earrings

them to shave their heads to conform to his own appearance. The order was intensely resented because it was customary to shave the heads and chins of criminals, and at Theophilus' death it was hurriedly annulled.

In later times rich men wore a great deal of jewelry, but those belonging to the working classes went barefoot even in winter. The rich wore long coats or caftans trimmed with a great deal of embroidery; some were lined with exquisite silks or, if intended for winter wear, with scarce and expensive furs. Under them they wore long tunics, whose long sleeves were gathered into embroidered cuffs. Poorer men wore shorter, often sleeveless tunics made of a woolen stuff, belted at the waist with a strap from the belt passing over their left shoulders.

Peasants wore cheap homemade versions of the townsmen's clothes. Their houses were small and unpretentious, consisting at most of two rooms. They were square or rectangular in shape and were built of wood, stone, or brick, depending on local custom. The lower story served as a stable, cattle shed, henhouse, wood store, and potting shed. The living quarters were on the upper floor and were reached by an external staircase. The better-off peasants kept a small garden, but this was a luxury. The villages were surrounded by orchards which contained fig trees and vines which were privately owned. A belt of fields lay beyond the orchards, and these were also privately owned, but the grazing land beyond belonged to all the villagers. A shepherd, either a child or an old person, would collect the animals every morning and lead them out to graze, bringing them back at night. The villagers seldom ate meat but lived off the cereals, vegetables, fruit, eggs, and milk which they had produced for the purpose. Byzantium was so often at war that villagers were not encouraged to travel much beyond their local market town. A police force existed to protect their fields, orchards, and animals against thieves, but all too often either an invading army or their own troops would sweep through the district ruining the crops which had been cultivated so laboriously. They would also make off with the poultry and cattle, leaving the peasants to face hunger and poverty as best they could.

CHAPTER FOUR

The Iconoclast Controversy

THROUGHOUT Byzantium's existence, regardless of whether *Relics* a person was rich or poor, busy or with time hanging heavy on his hands, happy and with many interests or depressed and bored, religion remained the most important thing in his life. Until the seventh century relics of saints and martyrs had greatly helped in encouraging this attitude, a development which Empress Helena had done much to establish by bringing a piece of the True Cross back to Constantinople from the Holy Land. Pilgrims to Palestine had kept interest in relics alive by also bringing some back to their native towns and villages and by presenting them to their local church or favorite monastery. Over the years Constantinople acquired a great many relics. Its inhabitants set particular store on what they believed to be the Virgin's robe and girdle. At Justinian's orders they were kept in the Church of St. Mary of the Blachernae, and people came to believe that the robe and girdle were able to protect Constantinople from danger. They therefore took to carrying them around the town's walls whenever an enemy threatened it.

The Byzantines also greatly revered the Sacred Mandelion, known to Europe as Veronica's kerchief, which, according to legend, had been placed over the face of the dead Christ and received the imprint of His features; the picture came to be known to the Orthodox as the likeness of "Christ Painted Not by Human Hands." Moses' staff ranked as another important relic, and there were scores of less famous ones, all of which were nevertheless passionately treasured. Some churches owned so many relics that they assembled them in a special building known as a martyrion; it was generally dedicated to the same saint as the church to which it belonged. On the anniversary of the saint's martyrdom a special service was held in the martyrion in his 73

honor. The custom dated back to Emperor Justinian, the builder of Constantinople's first martyrion; it took the form of a church rather than a chapel and was dedicated to the martyred saints Sergius and Bacchus. It is large and beautiful and is one of the finest of the early churches to survive in Istanbul.

The flow of relics from the Holy Land was very great. The church approved of them because they encouraged people to visit local shrines, martyrions, and the monasteries in which they were to be found. Then, toward the middle of the seventh century, the supply of relics suddenly ended. The reason for this event was dramatic and of lasting importance to the world as a whole. It was caused by a man called Mohammed who was born in Mecca in about the year 570. He was soon to rank as a prophet, for, on reaching manhood, Mohammed spent some fifteen years in trying exactly to understand the religious principles which he had learned from the Almighty and in clearly expressing them. When he had done so, he started to preach the faith known now as *Islamic*. Although he gained many followers, he also made many enemies. By 622 – the year which Moslems regard as the first in their history – Mohammed's enemies were so numerous and strong that he was obliged to fly from Mecca to avoid them. Fighting broke out soon after between him and his supporters and those who opposed them, but Mohammed and his followers proved victorious, and in 629 Mohammed was able to lead a pilgrimage to Mecca. In the following year he became ruler of Mecca, and at his death, two years later, his doctrine was adopted by the Arabs; Mecca was acknowledged as the holiest Islamic city because Mohammed had been born there. By founding a new religion, Mohammed completely changed the religious beliefs, mentality, and attitude to life of most Arabs within the space of ten years.

The rise of Islam

The first Moslems were filled with missionary zeal. They declared a holy war on all those unwilling to accept Mohammedanism and attacked those living nearest to their borders. They overran Persia first and then penetrated deep into southwestern Siberia. In 634 they attacked Byzantium. Led by Omar, Mohammed's father-in-law and the first caliph, or religious head of Islam, they invaded the provinces

The Arab conquests

(*Opposite*) A sumptuous gold and cloisonné enamel reliquary of the eleventh century, with later additions, for a fragment of the True Cross

which the Byzantines had recently been at such pains to win back from the Persians and headed for the Syrian border. The battle for Syria was fought and lost by the Byzantines at Jarmuk in the grueling heat of August, 636. The terrified inhabitants of Antioch hurried to surrender their rich and beautiful city in the hope of saving it from destruction, even though it meant placing themselves under Moslem rule.

There was worse to follow, for the Arabs now turned on the Holy Land. Inspired by their Patriarch, the people of Jerusalem proved more courageous than those of Antioch. They mustered in defense of their town, their religion, and their homes, but their bravery was not sufficient to halt the invaders. Jerusalem fell to the Arabs after a fiercely contested battle. For three days they looted the town, ill-treating and killing its inhabitants. Peace at any cost became the cry in certain sections of Byzantine society so that, even though the Arabs turned northward to attack Armenia, the widow of Emperor Heraclius, acting in the capacity of regent, opened peace talks with the Arabs and obtained a truce from them in return for the surrender of Egypt.

The Arab threat to Eastern Christendom For centuries to come, the Byzantines were to find it necessary to fight the Arabs in order to survive as Christians. At times they were even obliged to defend Constantinople from attacks launched by the Arabs both by sea and by land. Their success in repelling the naval attacks was largely due to their possession of a weapon of war, known as Greek fire, which gave them an immense advantage over their enemies for eight centuries, when it was rendered ineffective by the invention of firearms. Greek fire can best be described as the world's first grenade, for it consisted of a pottery case filled with saltpeter and various explosives which could be either hurled at the enemy or fired on him from a catapult. It had been invented toward the end of the seventh century by Callinicus, a Syrian architect who had escaped from Heliopolis when the Arabs invaded his country and had settled in Constantinople. Yet even with the aid of Greek fire, which they alone possessed, the Byzantines could do little more than protect Constantinople and Asia Minor from the Arabs. The Moslems retained the holy places, and it became difficult, at times even wholly impossible, for pilgrims to visit Palestine.

Shortly before the birth of Islam, as early perhaps as the fifth century and certainly by the sixth, Christians had started painting religious pictures which resembled the paintings decorating the inner walls of their churches. These portable religious works are known as icons; although the Greek word "icon" really meant a portrait, it came to be used for all figural works, especially for those painted on panels. The first religious paintings on wood closely resembled those of the tomb portraits produced in Egypt during the opening centuries of the Christian Era. An early icon of the Virgin was thought by the Byzantines to have been painted by St. Luke.

Justinian probably helped make icons popular when he adorned the altar screen in Hagia Sophia with the three *deësis* medallions. Soon after, icons were being used in churches, for although the walls of the richer ones were already covered with painted or mosaic scenes, the icons helped increase their numbers. In the poorer churches they often provided the only pictures of the Holy Family and of the main events in their lives. When the supply of relics ended, following the Arab conquest of Palestine, icons acquired a deeper meaning for the worshipers. They were soon being displayed in the churches on lecterns, and worshipers could approach very much nearer to them than they could to the wall paintings. As a result, a bond formed between the worshiper and the icon, and although icons were never taken for exact portraits of the people represented on them, they were nevertheless accepted as their likenesses. The saints shown on them were therefore given distinct, clearly recognizable features. Worshipers came to feel that the icon could serve as a sort of go-between and would help them induce the saints to whom they addressed their prayers to intercede for them with the Almighty. All understood the need not to mistake icons for idols.

The difference between an icon and an idol was a very definite one and, at any rate at first, clear-cut, for the worshiper knew that he was addressing his prayers to the being represented on the icon, not to the icon itself. Nevertheless, people gradually came to believe that certain icons possessed miraculous powers, and when that happened, the distinction between an icon and an idol became blurred. By

Two foot soldiers of the tenth century

the eighth century icons were being worshiped with such intensity that some people started to feel concerned. They were perhaps influenced by an old belief current in the East and shared by Jews and Moslems alike that it was wrong to include the human figure in a religious work of art, especially in the case of a divine or saintly being.

Byzantium's military position had steadily worsened since Justinian's death. Many of the conquests he had made both in the East and in the West had proved short-lived. The appearance of new enemies, new concentrations of power, new outlooks and ambitions had threatened them from the start. Within four years of his death the Lombards had invaded Italy and were so successful that their victories encouraged the Visigoths to embark on the conquest of Spain. To make matters worse certain Asian people, especially the Avars and Bulgars, had entered Europe and established themselves in what are now southern Russia and Bulgaria, while the Slavs had begun to pit their strength against Byzantium's. During the seventh century Byzantium had often been obliged to fight one or other of these people while retaining the bulk of its army in the East to guard its territory from the Arabs. *Byzantium's new enemies*

In 717 Leo III became emperor. On taking stock of the military and political situations, he saw that Byzantium was in an acutely dangerous position. He tried to discover the cause of his country's weakness for he thought that there must be some explanation for the humiliating military defeats of the preceding century and also for the political unrest which had disrupted life within Byzantium during the past twenty years or so. He came to the conclusion that these misfortunes must have been visited on the Byzantines by the Almighty as a punishment for their wrongdoings. The more he thought about it, the more convinced he became that the wrongs which were being punished with such severity could be none other than the excessive adoration which so many of his subjects were lavishing on icons.

Leo's belief that icons were being wrongly worshiped led him to think that it was also wrong for the human figure to be included in religious works of art. Many eminent people shared his view, and in 726, Leo therefore gave orders for the painting of Christ decorating the Chalke Gate, the *Iconoclasm* main and therefore the grandest gate in his palace, to be removed and replaced by one of the cross. The order marked the start of a quarrel which was to rage in Byzantium for more than 100 years. It is known as the iconoclast controversy because it took place between the iconoclasts, or image haters, and the iconodules, or image lovers.

Although the removal of the painting of Christ from the top of the Chalke Gate aroused strong opposition, nothing very definite occurred till 730, when Leo issued an edict forbidding the inclusion of the human figure in religious works of art. The Patriarch of Constantinople protested against this order so strongly and openly that Leo lost his temper and removed him from his office. However, the Patriarch's views were widely supported by the working classes, all of whom were deeply attached to icons. They were also upheld by St. John of Damascus, one of the outstanding theologians of the day, who, although living in Arab-controlled territory, was highly esteemed in Byzantium. Later St. Theodore, the distinguished abbot of the Studite Monastery in Constantinople, was also to support the use of icons and of figural representations in religious art. Their attitude was upheld in Europe. In Rome, first Pope Gregory II, then his successor Gregory III, firmly opposed the emperor's edict, expressing themselves as strongly as had the Patriarch of Constantinople. On finding that the emperor intended to ignore their protests, the latter Pope publicly proclaimed the Catholic Church sovereign and refused to submit to the emperor's authority.

Breach between the two churches   This action might perhaps have proved only temporary, had not Byzantium's inability to prevent the Lombards from capturing Ravenna in 751 led the Pope to seek a stronger protector, preferably one living in Western Europe. Pope Leo III was to find him in Charlemagne, whom he crowned Emperor of the West in Rome on Christmas Day, 800. By allowing Charlemagne to adopt that title, the Pope and the new monarch were openly challenging the Emperor of Byzantium's claim that as the successor of Rome's Caesars and also as Christ's vicar on earth, only the ruler of Byzantium was entitled to the supreme title of emperor. Charlemagne's coronation caused a deep breach between Byzantium and the West. The Orthodox Church felt

80

especially aggrieved by the Pope's refusal to recognize the Byzantine Emperor's right to enforce his wishes on the Church and thought that the Pope was acquiring greater authority over Western Europe than the Patriarch of Constantinople.

The iconoclast controversy raged with rising passion. The fiercer it grew, the worse did the emperor's relations become both with the papacy and with many influential Orthodox prelates. In the Arab-controlled East, Christians rallied around St. John of Damascus till he became the leader of a large and vocal opposition. Neither its strength nor its size had any effect on Leo III's son, Emperor Constantine V. The new emperor may possibly have thought that the victories which he had recently won over the Arabs were a sign of the Almighty's approval of his father's iconoclast policy, for he carried that policy even further than his father had done. He ordered all figural religious works, even those hallowed by age and tradition, to be destroyed. Defying the patriarchs of Antioch and Alexandria, he relentlessly pursued the iconodules, severely punishing, torturing, and killing those who fell into his hands. His cruelty and ruthlessness were not without effect, at any rate in Constantinople, where people began submitting to his wishes.

Constantine's son, Emperor Leo IV (775-80), was a kindlier man. Though he was also a staunch iconoclast and, as such, a maintainer of the ban on figural representations in religious art, he put an end to the persecution of the iconodules. His wife, Empress Irene, went further. On becoming regent at Leo IV's death in 780, she publicly expressed her sympathy with the iconodules and it was at her wish that the Church Council which met at Nicaea in 787 lifted the ban imposed on icons, allowing them to be used on condition that they were revered, but not adored.

The iconodules were triumphant, but not for long. Ten years later a revolution brought to the throne a new ruler who restored the ban. It was lifted in 811 by his son-in-law, Emperor Michael I Rhangabe (811-13), who had acted on the advice of his former tutor, Theodore, abbot of the Studite Monastery. Almost immediately the nation met with a series of major political and military reverses. The worst happened in 812, when, in order to keep the commercially

Military and political setbacks

F

valuable Venetian islands, the emperor was obliged to recognize Charlemagne as Emperor of the West. The defeat of his army by the Bulgars shortly afterward was far more serious, but worse still was to follow, for on hearing full details of the scale of that defeat, the Constantinopolitans rebelled. They deposed Michael and proclaimed one of their commanders Emperor Leo v. This time it was the people who ascribed the country's misfortunes to the Almighty's decision to punish them. They flocked to the tomb of Constantine v, the most ruthless of all iconoclasts, and forgetting his cruelty, they called on him to rise and defend them from the invincible King Krum of Bulgaria. Leo v hurriedly reimposed the ban on icons in the hope of calming his subjects. Although order was restored, Leo never won the trust of his people, nor did he prosper. Five years later he was murdered on Christmas Day by one of his former fellow commanders.

Lifting of iconoclast ban The new Emperor, Michael ii of the Amorians or Phrygians (820-29) maintained the ban on icons, but the decision did not bring him luck. It was during his nine-year reign that the Arabs captured the island of Crete and the valuable ports of Taormina in Sicily and of Bari in southern Italy. His son, Theophilus (829-42), was not content to let matters rest and revived the persecution of the iconodules, though limiting it largely to Constantinople. Shortly after his death, however, the ban was again lifted, this time permanently. The law legalizing the use of icons and of figural representations in religious art was welcomed. The announcement was celebrated on March 1, 843, by a service of great magnificence conducted in the Cathedral of Hagia Sophia by the Patriarch of Constantinople in the presence of the emperor and empress, their courts, and a large congregation. The event continues to be commemorated to-day by the Orthodox Church at a service called the Triumph of Orthodoxy held on the first Sunday in Lent.

The lifting of the iconoclast ban had an invigorating effect on the nation. In the military sphere it encouraged the army to fight the Moslems with such vigor that they won a number of valuable victories. In church circles it served to encourage missionary activities. The two saintly brothers, Cyril and Methodius, undertook a mission to the Khazars living on the lower reaches of the Volga River. On failing to convert them from Judaism, they went to Moravia and persuaded the Moravians to accept Orthodoxy. Then they invented an alphabet suited to the Slavonic languages. It was called the Cyrillic in their honor and was used by the various Slavonic nations as the basis for their individual alphabets as they became converted to Christianity. By joining the Orthodox Church, they drew closer to the Byzantine Church and thus to Byzantium, but their alphabets enabled each of these countries to create its own theological literature and to develop independently of the others and of Byzantium.

In Byzantium the defeat of iconoclasm proved stimulating to intellectuals. Interest revived in the works of Plato. Although the Church disapproved of this trend, Plato continued to be widely read because his theories provided arguments which could be used in support of a mystical philosophy popular at the time.

Byzantium's second golden age

Artists and craftsmen were even more strongly affected than most people by the repeal of iconoclasm, for it fired them with new ideas. They seemed inspired and, with the encouragement of a dynasty of emperors known as the Macedonian, they created so many works of outstanding quality that the period is often referred to as Byzantium's second golden age. Much of their output continued to be religious in character, hardly differing in form or composition from those used in earlier times, but the spirit which the posticonoclast artists infused into their works, especially into the paintings, is very different from that found in those which were produced in Justinian's day. All trace of Roman influence has disappeared from these later works. The Byzantine elements appear in them clear-cut and supreme. The painted and glass mosaic scenes are grand in conception, even when their actual size is far from being so; they are serene, assured, vigorous, and majestic, yet delicate. Those of a wholly decorative character are exquisite, inventive, and equally accomplished. Although the churches were smaller than in Justinian's day, they were often roofed by three domes, sometimes by five, and seemed slenderer and taller as a result. Icons, however, became larger, grander, and far more numerous. The ban had not greatly altered the people's attitude toward them. They continued to believe that some icons possessed the power to work miracles, that each one could help make a worshiper's prayers clearly heard in heaven. As late as the eleventh century, Romanus III (1028-34) made a practice of taking a miracle-working icon of the Virgin with him when he led his troops into battle.

However, the restoration of icons did not help the Orthodox and Catholic churches to come to a better understanding. In fact, the reverse happened, for Cyril and Methodius' success in converting first the Moravians and then the Bulgarians had strengthened the Byzantine Church, and as a result, Rome had become resentful. Both the Pope and Photius, Patriarch of Constantinople, wanted his own post recognized as senior in rank. When dealing with theological matters, their arguments therefore became increasingly personal in tone. Their mutual dislike and jealousy made both so bitter, that one day the Pope angrily accused Photius of having incorrectly interpreted certain religious texts. Then, in 863, he attempted to force the emperor to depose the patriarch. Photius retaliated by publicly proclaiming the Pope a heretic.

Separation of the two churches   In 867 the Holy Synod, the assembly of priests charged with the conduct of the affairs of the Orthodox Church, brought matters to a head at a meeting in council under the emperor's presidency by excommunicating the Pope. Contacts between the two churches were broken off. Emperor Basil I (867-86) made matters worse on coming to the throne, for in an attempt to please the Pope, he deposed Photius and exiled him to a monastery. Completely misjudging the nation's feelings, he then allowed the Pope's legate publicly to excommunicate the disgraced patriarch. This caused so much resentment in Byzantium that in 873 the emperor tried to make amends by bringing Photius back to Constantinople to become tutor to his sons. Four years later, when the patriarchate fell vacant, Basil restored Photius to his former position and persuaded the Pope to recognize the appointment. Diplomatic relations were restored between the two churches, but they lacked cordiality. The breach which had been created was never healed; indeed, it widened in the eleventh century, and in 1054 the two branches of the

84   Christian Church decided to separate and go their own ways.

CHAPTER FIVE

The Four Crusades

BYZANTIUM's territory had shrunk considerably soon after *Territorial* Justinian's death. In the seventh century large areas of *losses* Italy fell to the Lombards, the whole of Spain to the Visigoths, and Palestine, Syria, and Egypt to the Arabs. At the same time the Serbs and Croats had begun to break away from the large community of Slavs who had been slowly migrating from the neighborhood of the Vistula River since the end of the sixth century.

While they were settling in what are now Serbia and *Rise of Bulgaria* Croatia, other groups of Slavs had moved southward and raided Athens, but many more had joined the Bulgars, an Asian people who had advanced westward and had by then established themselves in what is now Bulgaria. Their joint forces attacked Byzantium for the first time in 678 but were beaten back. They tried again in 713 and on this occasion succeeded in reaching the walls of Constantinople but were unsuccessful in taking the city. They withdrew to Bulgaria, where they founded their first kingdom. It proved a constant threat to Byzantium's security.

Meanwhile, another large group of Asian warriors, the Avars, had formed a huge kingdom of their own just to the east and north of the Bulgarian; they too started frequently to raid Byzantium's territory.

To the northeast of the Avars the eastern Slavs, the *Rise of Russia* ancestors of the Russians, were living in small groups along the banks of the great rivers which flow across southwestern Russia. Under the leadership of Norse chieftains they had by the ninth century formed themselves into principalities; their princes recognized the supreme authority of the Grand Duke of the duchy of Kiev. Their combined territories formed a country which was known at the time as Rus and which later expanded, first into Muscovy, then into Russia, 85 and is now the USSR. In 866 the Rhos, as its inhabitants were called, crossed the Black Sea, landed on Byzantine soil, and marched to the very walls of Constantinople. They did not stay long, for the expedition had been planned as a raid, rather than as a campaign, but they returned home laden with booty. The venture had proved so profitable that the Rhos raided Byzantium more than once. In 907 they besieged Constantinople and hung their shields on its walls. The Byzantines obtained their withdrawal by granting them valuable trading rights in Constantinople, but the Rhos remained dangerous neighbors till 988, when Vladimir, Grand Duke of Kiev, decided to adopt Orthodoxy as his own and his people's religion. By doing so, he was able to marry no less a person than the sister of the Emperor of Byzantium, and from having been Byzantium's enemy, Rus became the empire's friend.

Bulgarians besiege Constantinople
Basil I (867-86), the founder of Byzantium's great Macedonian dynasty, could not stop fretting over Byzantium's lost territories. Although he still retained small areas of southern Italy and practically the whole of Sicily, he felt bound, as Justinian had done three centuries earlier, to try to reconquer them. After spending many months in difficult and exhausting fighting, he succeeded in winning back several districts in southern Italy, but his gains were offset by the loss of Sicily and Malta. His son, Leo VI, has gone down in history as Leo the Wise, yet he was foolish enough to quarrel with Simeon, the warrior King of Bulgaria. Their disagreement resulted in a war which continued to rage after Leo's death. The Bulgarians steadily gained the upper hand in the fighting and were able once again to lay siege to Constantinople. Byzantine casualties were extremely heavy, yet they managed to hold out, and the Bulgarians eventually withdrew to their own country. Although the campaign left Byzantium's frontiers little changed, it had given the Bulgarians control over the Balkans; they were to retain it till early in the eleventh century.

Emperor Basil II (976-1025) determined to avenge his country's honor by becoming master of the Balkans again. In 1001 he declared war on the Bulgarians. The contest was fierce and long drawn out, for it was not till 1014 that Basil managed to trap the main Bulgarian army in the Struma

Valley. Although they had little chance of breaking free, the Bulgarians fought heroically to do so. By nightfall thousands had died and 14,000 had been taken prisoner. Basil was determined to teach them a lesson they would never forget and resorted to extreme measures for the purpose. He divided the prisoners into groups of 100, tying each man to his neighbor. Then, as the groups were led forward in turn, he had the eyes of all but the first prisoner put out. After that Basil sent the blinded men back to their king at Prilep. When they presented themselves before him, their appearance was so terrible that the king fell into a deep faint and died of a broken heart two days later.

Even so, the Bulgarians fought on for another four years, and it was not until 1018 that Basil was able to enter their town of Ohrid (Ochrida) in triumph to annex Bulgaria. By then the emperor had become known to the world as Basil the Bulgar Slayer, but although he had brought the first Bulgarian kingdom to an end, he did not behave harshly or ungenerously when peace had been restored. Indeed, he granted the conquered Bulgarians more political freedom than most conquerors gave their victims, nor did he interfere with their intellectual activities. As a result, Bulgaria's cultural life continued to develop, even though the country had lost its independence.

While all this had been happening in the West, the Arabs had continued to harass the Byzantines in the East. Every spring was likely to bring with it an Arabian invasion of Anatolia. The peasants suffered most from these raids, yet the emperors often increased their taxes in order to raise the funds needed by their armies. The cost of financing wars on several fronts was enormous. The country's treasury was often empty, yet it did not seem to occur to any of the emperors to reduce their personal expenses. Life in Constantinople went on as in happier days, and at court the ceremonial was as magnificent and as elaborate as in earlier times.

The eastern wars

The fighting in the East settled very little. Sometimes one side won a victory or two, sometimes the other. Sometimes a truce would make life a little easier for the long-suffering peasants, but then either the Arabs or the Byzantines would attack again, though the gains that either made were small. 87

However, toward the middle of the tenth century, Emperor Romanus Lecapenus (920-44) recaptured Edessa and some outlying districts. At Edessa he was able to recover from the enemy the miraculous icon of "Christ Painted Not by Human Hands." The Byzantines were as delighted by this as by the military achievement. The icon was carefully carried back to Constantinople to enter the capital in triumph in 944, at the head of a magnificent procession.

The advantage won over the Moslems by Romanus Lecapenus was maintained by Basil the Bulgar Slayer. Although he had concentrated the bulk of his forces in Bulgaria, he still managed to build up Byzantium's position in the East. At his death it seemed that the situation there had become stable. Respect for Byzantium revived, for although the country was smaller than in Justinian's day, it was once again strong enough to defend itself from powerful enemies attacking it on various fronts.

Admiration for Byzantium was not solely based on Basil II's military victories, but was also partly inspired by the remarkable revival of scholarship and the art under the Macedonian Dynasty. The country's future seemed bright with promise in 1057, when the throne passed to Isaac Comnenus.

The nomads of central Asia Yet as Isaac mounted the throne, a new and far more serious threat to Byzantium's existence than any the country had as yet had to face developed in the northeast. From ancient times, the immense central Asian plain had belonged to various nomadic tribes, who lived by rearing their herds of cattle and horses on its grazing lands. Many of these tribes were of Turkish origin. In the sixth century after Christ some had formed a kingdom on the banks of the Oxus (Amu Darya) River, but in the eighth century the Arabs had penetrated into the area and ended its existence. Now the Turkish tribes were massing again; several had set up kingdoms of their own in parts of present-day Afghanistan and in northwestern Persia. By the eleventh century the tribe of the Seljuk Turks had become one of the most powerful among them.

The Byzantines had ignored these developments and allowed themselves to be swept by a wave of pacifism. They had never been a warlike people and had always been more interested in religion, philosophy, and the arts than in fighting battles. Many emperors had as a result been obliged to rely on mercenaries for the men they needed for their armies. Now the Byzantines were tired of war and bloodshed; they took no interest in their army and allowed it to run down; they failed to notice that their fortifications were falling into disrepair. The emperor shared their pacifist outlook, and there was no one at court or in the administration to draw his attention to the dangers which face a disarmed state. No one realized that the Seljuks were steadily marching westward. Even when they had conquered Persia, captured Baghdad, and become converted to Mohammedanism, the Byzantines remained blind to the danger signals. They made no attempt to rearm or to prepare themselves for war.

The Seljuks reached the borders of Fatimid Egypt in 1064. There they split up, and while one group marched on Syria, the other turned on Armenia. They were a race of warriors and now seemed as invincible as the Arabs had done some four centuries earlier. Like the Arabs, they were not impressed by Byzantium's size and military reputation and did not hesitate to start raiding its border lands. They did so every spring, each time penetrating deeper into Byzantium and inflicting ever heavier losses on its inhabitants. It began to look as if the Seljuks, not the Byzantines, owned these districts. In Constantinople people started to feel angry and concerned.

In 1068 a distinguished and experienced professional soldier called Romanus Diogenes became emperor. Though he realized the extent of Byzantium's military weakness, he appreciated the danger in which the Seljuks had placed the country. He could not ignore public opinion in his capital nor the right of his subjects living in the eastern provinces to be defended from the Seljuk raiders. He would have to fight the Seljuks. He began at once to start repair work on the country's more important fortifications. He also set himself to make good the shortage in arms, to hire as many mercenaries as possible to fight in his armies, and especially to find competent officers to command and keep them in order. By means of almost ceaseless work and effort he managed to put an army in the field in the following spring. He took personal command and managed to defend his boundaries

The Seljuk wars

against the Seljuk raiders. He did equally well in the following year. Encouraged by these small achievements, he decided to mount a major campaign in the spring of 1071. In the hope of destroying the Seljuks, he engaged more mercenaries than usual with the result that although his army was larger than the first two, it was also less well disciplined and trained.

The Battle of Manzikert It may have been due to the inefficiency of some of the emperor's officers rather than to an error on his part that when he led his men to the Persian border, no scouts were sent to spy out the land or to gain information about the enemy's movements. The omission was to have the gravest results. Alp Arslan, Sultan of the Seljuks, was fully informed about the emperor's activities. On discovering Romanus Diogenes' position, he set out to trap the Byzantines in the valley of Manzikert in the district of Erzurum.

On the morning of Friday, August 18, 1071, he put his plan into effect. It was not until the entire Byzantine Army had entered the valley that the emperor discovered that they were bottled up in it and had either to surrender or to try to fight their way out. When they saw what had happened, most of the Turkoman and Turkish mercenaries in his service deserted to join forces with Alp Arslan. Nevertheless, the Byzantine Army still outnumbered the Seljuk forces, and all might yet have gone well. But the Latin mercenaries decided to be neutral and withdrew to a hill from which they could watch the fighting. Their departure and the ferocity of the Seljuk attack unnerved the Byzantines. They forgot to guard their emperor and broke up into small groups. Most fought courageously, but their resistance was ineffective.

Many died in the battle; the remainder, including the emperor, were taken prisoner. The defeat was so shattering that the Byzantines were never able to speak of the battle other than as "that dreadful day." Though they ransomed their emperor for half a million dinars, they had to accept bitter peace terms; they had to release all the Moslem prisoners whom they had captured over the years and to promise to supply the Seljuks with Byzantine troops whenever asked to do so. In return they obtained a truce, but despite this, civil war broke out in Byzantium when these harsh conditions became known. Romanus Diogenes was deposed, blinded, and sent into exile to die of a broken heart within a year.

Alp Arslan was well aware that his victory had opened the door to Anatolia for him, but he died before he could lead his army there. Suleiman, his successor, decided against an immediate attack and contented himself with making preparations for war. Luck was on his side, for the Byzantine throne had passed to the scholarly Michael Dukas Parapinakes, who was a pacifist. Appalled by the magnitude of the Seljuk threat, by his lack of a reliable army, by his unfitness to deal with so difficult a situation, he ignored the ill feeling which marred Byzantium's relations with Rome and appealed to the Pope for military aid. The Pope failed to appreciate just how serious the situation in the East had become and took no action. Distracted, Michael tried to raise an army for himself by enrolling anyone willing to serve in it. A Norman baron called Roussel of Bailleul was among those who volunteered. He did so more because of a desire to become rich and powerful than out of concern for Eastern Christians. He set himself to win Michael's trust, and having done so, he proceeded to abuse it. Although he had sworn allegiance to the emperor, he did not hesitate to seize a large area of Anatolia for himself when the chance came. Proclaiming it his principality, he appealed to Suleiman, Michael's most dangerous enemy, for help in retaining it. The sultan was only too delighted to agree, and the Islamic invader and the Christian traitor became allies in an attempt to destroy Byzantium.

Rebellions flared up throughout Byzantium. A rival emperor appeared demanding the throne. Driven by fear, Michael followed the example of Roussel of Bailleul and appealed to Sultan Suleiman for help in restoring order. Suleiman was delighted since every chance to intervene increased his strength and reputation. Again luck was on his side, for the Seljuks were able to take Roussel prisoner. Suleiman had no hesitation in offering to cede the Norman to the emperor in return for a large ransom. Michael agreed to pay it. In the face of situations such as these, the political unrest grew worse, leader after leader appealing in turn to Suleiman for help. By agreeing to all their requests, the

The Seljuk threat

Seljuk steadily edged his way deeper into Byzantium till he had annexed Lydia and Ionia. In 1078 he was able to proclaim Nicaea his capital. The city had long been closely linked with the Christian Church; its fall came as a shock to Europeans. Worse was to come. Suleiman's kingdom was soon to extend to the Mediterranean in the southwest and to Syria in the east. Christians living in the conquered areas were bereft of hope.

Alexius
Comnenus Byzantium was now faced with economic disaster. People despaired of the future and felt utterly lost when a man came forward to save them from further misrule. He was called Alexius Comnenus and belonged to Byzantium's ancient military aristocracy. He had fought for his country on several occasions, always displaying both courage and initiative. He seized the throne on Easter Sunday, 1081; his descendants were to retain it till 1185 and were to reign with such ability that life was once again to seem rich and full of promise; art and learning were to experience another period of intense creativeness. However, these happy conditions lay concealed in the future, and few would have been bold enough to foretell them when Alexius took over the country. The Comnene achievement itself was to prove short-lived – a mere interlude – and it was as well that the ultimate disappointment also lay concealed from those who acclaimed the new emperor on that Easter Sunday.

The situation facing Alexius was indeed bleak. Not only did the Seljuks hold most of Asia Minor, but in the West, the Normans were about to attack the Byzantines in Italy, and a fierce tribe of Asian nomads called Patzinaks were massing in the Balkans for a similar purpose. Alexius longed above all else to rid Byzantine of the Seljuks, but he realized that his army was not strong enough to do so and that it would therefore be wiser to use the available troops in defense of his Western territories. The Normans were recent arrivals in Italy. They had come there to serve the Lombards as mercenaries and had taken such a liking to the country that they had stayed on. Their chieftain, Robert Guiscard, now wanted to extend his possessions by taking advantage of Byzantium's difficulties to expel the Greeks from the eastern shores of the Adriatic Sea.

92 Alexius was desperately in need of men to serve in his

A marble slab from a twelfth century church showing a peacock

armies. He too had to rely largely on mercenaries, but even with their help his troops were not able to hold out against the Normans. It seemed to Alexius that the Pope was the only person able to help him raise more recruits. He therefore appealed to him for military aid in the form of volunteers for his armies, while at the same time trying his utmost to improve relations between the two churches. For ten years Rome had heard Byzantium's cries for help without paying much attention to them. Alexius' request also fell on unresponsive ears. On the verge of despair the emperor turned to the Venetian Republic for help. This seemed reasonable enough at the time, but it was to prove most unfortunate in the long run, for the Venetians' longing to own Constantinople was as a result to grow into an ungovernable passion. At the time, however, the alliance enabled the Venetian and Byzantine navies jointly to attack the Normans and decisively to defeat them. The Normans might perhaps have recovered from their losses had not a severe outbreak of plague killed many of those who remained. Robert Guiscard was among those who died of it in 1085. On finding themselves leaderless, the Normans gave up the contest and withdrew into Italy.

The war had severely taxed Byzantium's strength and resources, but the nation soon found itself obliged to face another trial of strength. In 1091 the Patzinaks attacked Constantinople by land while their Moslem allies did so by sea. The Constantinopolitans fought them in a white heat of fury. Their anger gave them the strength to smash the nomad force. The Patzinaks were broken and ceased to count as a dangerous enemy. On seeing their plight, the Moslem navies withdrew, leaving Alexius free to deal with the situation in Asia Minor in the knowledge that his western boundaries were safe, at any rate for the time being.

Pilgrims   Pilgrimages to the Holy Land had resumed after the Arabs had firmly established their control over Palestine, but the Seljuk victory at Manzikert had once again brought them to an end. At first Rome had not felt unduly concerned by the cutting of the pilgrim route to Jerusalem, but with each passing year would-be pilgrims were increasingly distressed by it. Therefore when, in 1095, Alexius once again appealed to the Pope for help, clearly stating that he needed it in the form of loyal and well-trained troops, the request received careful consideration. Rome had never given up hope of seeing the Papacy proclaimed senior in rank to the Patriarchate of Constantinople. Alexius' appeal gave these hopes fresh life. Thinking that the emperor might agree to make the desired pronouncement if he were provided with military aid, the Pope loudly appealed to Christendom to come forward in support of the Eastern Christians. On this occasion his words were listened to and answered, though not in accordance with Alexius' needs. The emperor's request for mercenaries willing to serve under Byzantine commanders was ignored. It is impossible to tell whether this was done on purpose or unintentionally, but the cry which resounded through Europe was for a holy war, a crusade. It spread across Western Christendom like a flame, firing the imagination of countless men. Some were genuinely inspired by a desire to save the Eastern Christians from their Moslem conquerors, but many joined the crusade in the hope of winning personal wealth and fame. In the general excitement no one remembered to notify or to consult the Byzantine Emperor about the plans which were
94 being made in the West.

Boats such as this one were used by travelers and inshore fishermen

In July, 1096, just as Alexius had completed the prepara- *The First* tions for a spring campaign against the Seljuks, men of *Crusade* Western nationality and Catholic faith started to arrive in Constantinople in a steady stream. By the end of the year their numbers had reached a very large figure, but the new arrivals seemed to expect to be housed, fed, and supported by the emperor. Yet they were not the trained and disci- plined soldiers Alexius had asked for; the majority of his uninvited guests were unruly men inexperienced in warfare. Shortly after their arrival they began to abuse the Con- stantinopolitans, looting their shops and houses and com- mitting other excesses. Appalled by their behavior, Alexius decided to ferry them across the sea to Asia, but soon after they had been landed there, the Seljuks fell upon them, killing most of them. Those who managed to escape made their way back to Constantinople, where they were soon joined by more Crusaders arriving from the West.

The leaders of this, the First Crusade, were among the last to reach Constantinople. They proved little better than their men. Though many came from Europe's most distinguished families, they seemed more anxious to enrich themselves than to free the Holy Land from Moslem control. The emperor found them insufferable, but he concealed his disgust and did his best to be a good host. Nevertheless, he decided to make them swear two oaths to him – an oath of personal loyalty and a promise to return to Byzantium any of its former territories which they managed to set free. The Latin princes needed a great deal of persuading, but at last they pledged themselves.

The First Crusade set out from Constantinople in the spring of 1097 and quickly captured Nicaea. It was a hopeful beginning, though tarnished by the Crusaders' attempts to loot the town. While the Byzantines turned westward to try to win back such important towns as Izmir, Ephesus, and Sardis, the Crusaders pushed eastward toward Antioch. The Seljuks tried to stop them by engaging them in battle in July at Dorylaeum. It was to prove a rare, but also their worst, defeat. The Christians compared their victory to the one which the Seljuks had won twenty years earlier at Manzikert, for it opened their road to Anatolia and enabled them to capture Kayseri and Konya with comparative ease. Antioch proved more difficult to overcome. It held out for many months but capitulated in June, 1098.

Their victories should have drawn the allies closer together, but the reverse happened, for each success increased the chances of winning richer prizes in the future, and the prospect of still greater gains fanned the personal ambitions and jealousies of the Crusade's leaders, while each quarrel increased their mutual distrust. Alexius saw his worst fears coming true when Baldwin, Count of Flanders, claimed Edessa for himself and then quarreled bitterly with Tancred, Prince of Sicily, over the possession of Tarsus. Meanwhile, Robert Guiscard's son, Bohemond, was having angry words with Raymond of Toulouse over

Antioch. The leaders of the Crusade forgot their Christian duty and their promises to the Emperor of Byzantium; they continued to wrangle over the division of spoils as they slowly marched toward the Holy Land, letting their men rob the towns and villages through which they passed. Nevertheless, the Crusaders reached Jerusalem at last. They laid siege to the town, capturing it in June, 1099. While most were celebrating their victory by plundering the town and killing many of its Jewish and Moslem inhabitants, Raymond of Toulouse stole a march on his fellow leaders by proclaiming himself King of Jerusalem.

The princes who had set themselves up as petty rulers of *The Latin* the conquered areas seemed not to notice that they had *kingdoms* broken faith with Emperor Alexius. But the Byzantines had a better memory. Hatred of the Latins flared up in their hearts. Realizing that he could not evict them by force, Alexius decided to make them quarrel among themselves. It is difficult to see what else he could have done, yet his policy was so much resented by the Latins that for centuries to come, they were apt to describe anyone who was "double tongued, mischievous and underhand" as Byzantine in behavior.

At Alexius' death the Latins controlled all the districts that had been captured from the Moslems, and Byzantium was no larger than it had been at the time of his coronation. Nevertheless, Alexius had given the country an efficient army which could stoutly defend its safety, and this had brought life back to normal for ordinary men and women. Although Byzantium had not benefited territorially from the Crusade, it had done so indirectly, for the Latin victory at Dorylaeum had greatly weakened the Seljuks, and the new Latin kingdoms in Syria and Palestine had turned Moslem attention away from Byzantium.

John II (1118-43), Alexius' son, therefore found himself the ruler of a healthy and hopeful country. He fully approved of his father's policy and took it as his own. He proved a worthy successor of Alexius, for he was able, upright, and persevering. He was also farsighted and among the first to sense the danger of Venetian domination. He tried to break free of the Republic, but by then too many Venetian merchants were living and working in Constantinople for this

G

to be possible. He did, however, stop the Serbians from forming themselves into a kingdom, but this meant he had to garrison an army in the Balkans to keep watch over them. The emperor had to raise another army in order to recover Antioch from the Latins. They were furious with him for doing so and tried to retake the town. They made it necessary for John to lead another army to Antioch's defense, but he died before reaching it, having been wounded by a poisoned arrow when out hunting.

His favorite son, Manuel, inherited his throne. Manuel was clever and brave and shared the political views of his father and grandfather. But although he adopted their policies, he also found much that appealed to him in the Latin way of life. He liked the greater freedom of Western court life and was especially attracted by the rules of chivalry governing Europe's knighthood. He delighted in tournaments and introduced jousting at his court, often even testing his own skill with the lance in a contest. Life at his court was more varied and amusing than in former times.

The Second Crusade Manuel's liking for Westerners was severely tested by the arrival in Constantinople in 1147 of the Second Crusade. The fact that it was led by King Louis VII of France and Conrad III, Emperor of Germany, alarmed the Byzantines, who thought that these rulers had designs on their territories. Their Latin soldiers proved no better behaved than those of the First Crusade. Like them, they ill-treated the people of Constantinople and were soon hated by them. Manuel was as anxious as his grandfather had been to prove a good host, but he was just as keen to rid himself of his uninvited guests. First, however, he insisted that they should swear to return to him the territories which they were able to liberate. The Crusaders intended to conquer Damascus, but their plans finally came to nothing; indeed, because of inefficiency, they were not even put to the final test.

Saladin and the Third Crusade The capture of Jerusalem by Saladin in 1182 from its Latin king led Europe to undertake the Third Crusade. It was to have been jointly commanded by King Richard of England, King Philip of France, and Frederick Barbarossa, Emperor of the Germans. But Frederick did not reach the Holy Land. He died of drowning in Asia Minor, having 98 fallen into a fast-flowing river which he was trying to cross.

The two remaining leaders continued their march for the purpose of engaging Saladin in battle. Emperor Isaac of Byzantium was, however, on good terms with Saladin, who was honorable and whose word could be trusted. Isaac had no desire to fight him and felt less troubled by the situation in the East than by that in the Balkans, where the Bulgarians and Serbs were fighting for their sovereignty. He therefore concentrated his forces in Europe, where he succeeded in driving the Bulgarians out of Thrace and the Serbians out of Macedonia. Though victorious, the peace treaty which followed accorded Serbia its sovereignty. It was confirmed by the marriage of Isaac's niece to the Serbian prince.

The happy ending to the Balkan war did not solve Isaac's difficulties, for his own relatives were undermining his position; members of his own family coveted his crown. The Venetians were involved in the intrigue, for they hoped to gain control of Constantinople's valuable eastern trade by siding with Isaac's brother, Alexius. With this end in view they encouraged rivalry between the two brothers, and it was their help which enabled Alexius to depose Emperor Isaac in 1195. On assuming the crown, Alexius III forgot all brotherly feelings and had Isaac blinded and banished to a monastery. Alexius proved an incompetent weakling. He was largely responsible for bringing his country to the verge of collapse at the very time when events in the West required that it should be strong and united. *Venetian intrigues*

The political pattern which had been built up in Europe over the centuries was completely disrupted when Henry VI of Germany suddenly inherited the kingdom of Sicily. The strategic advantages of inheriting Sicily led Henry, ambitious by nature, to covet an Eastern as well as a Western empire. He realized that he would have to conquer Byzantium to make his wish come true. Mischievously the Venetians did their best to encourage Henry to claim the Byzantine throne. Though he had no right to it, Henry demanded the Byzantine throne on the grounds that his brother's marriage to a daughter of the deposed Emperor Isaac entitled him to it. The claim was an empty one, but it terrified Emperor Alexius. Panicking, he offered to buy Henry off, but the German Emperor haughtily refused even to consider the idea. *Henry VI of Germany and Sicily*

The Pope had been keeping a close watch on the situation.

Believing it to be highly undesirable that Henry should reign over Byzantium in addition to Germany and Sicily, he intervened; ordering Henry to abandon all thought of annexing Byzantium, the Pope advised Henry to content himself with the money which Alexius had offered him and ordered him to atone for his arrogance by joining the Crusade to the Holy Land which the French were assembling. Henry felt obliged to comply.

The Fourth Crusade   Venice's affairs were directed at the time by Enrico Dandolo. Though old and blind, he was one of Venice's most remarkable rulers, or doges. Over the years he had managed to gain control of the Mediterranean and had steadily tightened his grip on Constantinople. He decided that the moment had come to attempt to annex the town; all that he needed was a pretext. The Fourth Crusade was to provide it. Its members had planned to make their way to Palestine by sailing from Venice to Egypt in Venice's large and comfortable ships, but by the time they reached Venice most of them had run out of money. The Doge told them that if they did not pay their fares, he would not ferry them – unless they first helped him capture the port of Zara from the King of Hungary. Since the king was a fellow Christian and had taken part in a Crusade the Pope was shocked by the suggestion and refused to sanction it, but the Crusaders agreed to the Doge's terms. The inhabitants of Zara were no match for the joint force of Venetians and Crusaders. Sooner than submit to them, the majority preferred to die defending their town, and only a handful survived the siege; Zara fell to the Latins in November, 1202.

It was not until the following May that the Fourth Crusade finally sailed from Venice. Its destination was no longer Egypt, for Doge Dandolo had persuaded Boniface de Montferrat to accept him as joint leader of an expedition which was to sail for Constantinople. The Venetian armada reached the walls of Constantinople on May 24 and instantly besieged the city. The district of Galata on the east bank of the Golden Horn belonged to the Latin community and so quickly surrendered. The invaders could then destroy the boom guarding the entrance to the Golden Horn and sail up the inlet in order to attack the town from the rear, while the Crusaders, who had been landed on the Marmora's shores, did so by land. The Byzantine troops, especially the emperor's Varangian, or Norse, bodyguard, supported by the civilian population fought them heroically, but Alexius III, the reigning emperor, deserted. He escaped from the town, taking the crown jewels and state funds with him. The defenders were greatly outnumbered, yet they would probably have held out had the Golden Horn remained closed to the enemy's ships. As matters stood, Constantinople, the town which was both the loveliest capital of its time and the one which was even more representative of Christianity than Rome, was obliged to surrender to a band of fellow Christians on July 17, 1203.

To begin with, the Venetians had an eye for the decencies of politics and concealed their personal ambitions. They obliged the Crusaders to keep to the camps which had been set up for them outside the capital's walls, they released the old and blind Emperor Isaac from exile and replaced him on his throne, but they also appointed his son, another Alexius, co-ruler and made both emperors their tools, obliging them to govern the country as their puppets.

The Constantinopolitans could not forgive Alexius IV for having urged a Latin army to conquer their city and rebelled. They marched on the palace, seized and killed Alexius, deposed his father, and locked him in a prison cell, where he soon died. They replaced their unworthy rulers with a man who shared their hatred of the Latins – Alexius Ducas. It seemed to the watching Latins that their prize was slipping through their fingers. Before Alexius Ducas had had time to assume control of affairs, they hastened to launch another attack on Constantinople. The citizens were willing, indeed anxious, to fight back, but the emperor knew that it was hopeless and insisted on asking the Latins for peace terms. The conditions demanded by the invaders were so harsh that on hearing them, the capital's inhabitants seized their weapons and rushed to man the town's defenses. The battle for Constantinople was fought for a second time. Although the defenders were greatly outnumbered, they held out until April 13, 1204.

The Latin entry into the subdued city on that day was to rank as an unforgettable disaster in the annals of the Orthodox world. It was also a grievous one for European culture. Constantinople had grown into a veritable treasure house of art and learning. Over the centuries great masterpieces and magnificent books had been assembled there till they had come to represent all that was best in the Christian civilization. For 1,000 years these wonderful collections had escaped harm. None had suffered at the hands of the various armies which had at one time or another besieged Constantinople. Yet all were to be destroyed or lost in the course of the next three days. In order to satisfy their men, the leaders of the Fourth Crusade handed the town over to them to do with as they liked during the next seventy hours. The soldiers who had set out to defend the Eastern Christians proved ruthless. They killed many of the town's inhabitants and ill-treated others; they destroyed countless buildings; they desecrated the cathedrals and churches, making off with their relics; they stole, smashed, or burned the priceless works of art and irreplaceable books.

A Byzantine historian sadly remarked that "even the Saracen are merciful and kind when compared with those who wear the cross of Christ on their shoulders."

CHAPTER SIX

The Turkish Invaders

ENRICO Dandolo, Doge of Venice, must be held responsible for the capture of Constantinople by Western Christians, for the outrages which took place there, and for the dismemberment of the Byzantine Empire. Although the conquerors appointed six Latins and six Venetians to elect a new emperor, it was the Doge's favorite, Count Baldwin of Flanders and Hainault, who was awarded the prize. On May 16 he was crowned ruler of the Latin Kingdom of Constantinople in the Cathedral of Hagia Sophia; the ceremony was performed by Thomas Morosini, the Venetian cleric chosen to become the first Latin Patriarch of Constantinople. Baldwin's share of Byzantium was half that retained by Venice and equal to the area which was divided into fiefs or principalities and allotted to various Latin knights. Those who received land in Greece grew rich and powerful, but they were outmatched by the French who created an *outre France* in Achaea and Morea under the leadership of William de Champlitte and Geoffrey de Villehardouin the Younger. Constantinople was also split up, the Venetians obtaining three-eighths of the town, while the rest formed Baldwin's capital.

The Byzantines detested their new masters because they came as conquerors, because they were arrogant and because they were members of the Catholic Church. Though the majority had to accept them, many others refused to do so. Shortly before the fall of Constantinople two grandsons of Andronicus I, Alexius and David Comnenus, had founded a kingdom of their own at Trebizond. Now many Byzantines tried to join them, while others followed their example. They included Michael Angelus, a member of the imperial family, who established himself as despot or ruler of Epirus in northern Greece, and Theodore Lascaris, a brother-in-law

The Latin Kingdom of Constantinople

103

of Emperor Alexius Angelus, who obtained possession of Nicaea. Proclaiming it his capital, he appointed Michael Autoreianus Patriarch and instructed the prelate to crown him Emperor of Byzantium. The Latins were not prepared to tolerate the existence of a Greek court and government and hurried to attack Nicaea before Theodore Lascaris had had time to deploy his small army in a favorable position. The battle was soon over, and Asia Minor seemed on the point of falling to the Latin victors.

The Nicaean Kingdom Suddenly, however, events in Thrace obliged the Latins to withdraw their troops from the East in order to use them against the Bulgarians, who had risen in support of the Byzantines. The two forces met in battle on the outskirts of Adrianople (Edirne) in April, 1205. Much more than the fate of that town depended on its outcome. Both sides knew this, and both therefore fought with terrible determination. By nightfall the victory belonged to the Slavs. Many Latins lay dead on the battlefield, and Baldwin was among the prisoners. The Bulgarians had saved Asia Minor for Theodore Lascaris; with Nicaea as his capital he set out to rival the Latins in Constantinople and eventually to evict them from it.

The Mongols Life had hardly settled down in the Nicaean kingdom before a new danger arose threatening to engulf Christendom. Once again it stemmed from Asia, from hordes of fierce, cruel, and invincible Mongols. Moving eastward, they were conquering everything in their path. Persia and Mesopotamia in the south and Rus in the north had already fallen to them, and the Seljuk sultanate of Iconium (Konya) was on the point of doing so. Theodore Lascaris' successor, John Vatatzes of Nicaea, realized that his turn would soon come. He tried to preserve his independence by entering into a defensive alliance in 1243 with the Sultan of Iconium, but on realizing that even their joint armies would not be able to stand out against the Mongols, he decided voluntarily to recognize their khan as his overlord. By doing so, he was able to pursue Theodore Lascaris' plan to liberate Constantinople and restore it to Byzantium. He began by retaking Thrace from the Bulgarians and Thessalonica from the despot of the Morea and was on the point of extending his campaign when he died of an epileptic fit. His son,

Emperor Theodore II Lascaris (1254-58), had inherited his father's love of scholarship and the arts so that, while culture stagnated in Latin-controlled Constantinople, it flourished in Nicaea. Theodore's death at the early age of thirty-six from an even worse epilepsy robbed the Nicaean kingdom of a great ruler. Theodore's son, John, was only seven when he inherited his father's throne. A regent took control, but he lacked the qualities essential to a ruler. His court became riddled with intrigue and corruption. Everything was on the point of being lost when Michael Paleologus seized control.

Michael Paleologus was one of the ablest, most patriotic, and most high-minded men at the Nicaean court. By birth a member of the ancient aristocracy, by profession a soldier, by marriage a relation of John Vatatzes, he possessed the valuable gift of knowing how to charm people. Within a year of seizing the regency he was elected to reign as co-emperor of young John IV. Like his predecessors on the Nicean throne, he too was determined to evict the Latins from Constantinople; unlike them, he was not prepared to wait. As a first step he captured Corfu; using the island as a naval base, he extended his control to the Greek coast. His success aroused the fears of the Latin princes. In order to destroy him, they formed a coalition which included the King of Sicily, but Michael challenged them by sending an army under the command of his brother John to engage them in battle. He had thrown all his troops into the contest. Each of his men knew that Byzantium's future depended on its outcome, and each was determined to fight to the last. The opposing armies met in the valley of Pelagonia in the autumn of 1259. The Byzantines fought so bravely that by the end of the day 400 Latin knights had died and many others had been taken prisoner. This victory was regarded as an omen by the Byzantines, for it promised the rebirth of their country. The Latins had suffered such a massive defeat that they were no longer a serious danger to the Byzantines.

The Venetians, however, were still powerful and dangerous. In order to strengthen his hand against them, Michael entered into an alliance with Genoa, Venice's chief rival and competitor in the Eastern trade. The Genoese later exacted a crippling payment from the Byzantines for their help, but

Michael the liberator

at first they contented themselves with a promise of commercial privileges, including tax concessions and customs benefits for their merchants and the gift of a district of their own in which to live in Constantinople and other major Byzantine ports.

The Latin Kingdom of Constantinople had been slowly decaying. Now it was rotten and ready to disintegrate. The commander of the small Byzantine force stationed in Thrace to guard the Bulgarian frontier suddenly discovered that Constantinople had been left virtually undefended. He did not pause to inform the emperor but hastened to lead his men in an attack on the capital. It met with little resistance, and the attackers succeeded in occupying Constantinople on the morning of July 22, 1261; their delight was slightly spoiled by their failure to capture Baldwin II, who had escaped with his courtiers shortly before the city's surrender.

Michael Paleologus made his triumphal entry to Constantinople as emperor of a free Byzantium on August 15. The event was of immense religious, political, and military importance and was celebrated with great solemnity. The emperor was met at the great Golden Gate – used only on ceremonial occasions – by a procession of dignitaries formed around the miraculous icon of the Virgin Hodegetria (Pointer of the Way) which served as the city's protective genius and was thought to have been painted by St. Luke. Dismounting from his splendidly caparisoned horse, the emperor went first to the Studite Monastery, where he gave thanks to God; then he proceeded to the Cathedral of Hagia Sophia, where a service of thanksgiving was held. His route was lined by a deliriously happy crowd. The great cathedral, which had served as the cradle of Orthodoxy, had reverted to its original faith. During the solemn, impressive service Michael was once again crowned emperor, this time of a free and united country. Shortly afterward he proclaimed his infant son, Andronicus, co-emperor, but then proceeded to mar his fine reputation by deposing young John Lascaris and having him blinded. Yet it was this cruel and unjustifiable act which enabled Michael to establish the great Paleologue Dynasty on Byzantium's throne. It was to be the last and the longest to reign in the country's history.

The artistic developments which took place under the Paleologi resulted in the creation of works of art of great splendor
and vigor. Although the country was too poor to sponsor the
creation of objects made of costly materials, the art of the
period attained a high degree of merit, the genius of
Byzantium's artists expressing itself as fully even when
mural paintings had to fill the place of costly glass mosaics
and pottery took the place of silver and gold. The capital
Michael had won back had been devastated. The Latins had
stripped it of everything of value, sparing neither church,
palace, nor private house. Few buildings which were not in
urgent need of major repairs had survived.

The emperor attempted to contain his enemies by diplo-   *Rise of the*
matic instead of military measures, playing the Venetians   *Ottoman Turks*
against the Genoese and Pisans in order to be able to use his
army to evict the Latin princelings who were holding out
in Greece. He was so deeply involved in these matters that
he ignored the various Turkish tribesmen who had entered
Byzantium in the wake of the Mongols. He did not seem to
notice that one tribe, the Ottoman, was already making its
home in Asia Minor. He continued to enroll Turks as

Head of Christ from a mural painting at
Kariye Djami, Istanbul, c 1330

mercenaries in the armies he needed for the fighting in the Peloponese, even though Tartar kinsmen of the Turks were massing in what is now southern Russia to attack Byzantium.

The emperor greatly needed the West's help, but he knew that it was useless to appeal to the Pope – unless he agreed to the union of the Latin and Orthodox churches. The idea of such a thing was hateful to the Byzantines, yet the emperor could see no other course but to agree to it. After many months spent in trying to win over his church-men, the emperor at last persuaded some of them to accept it and, on July 26, 1274, at the Council of the Churches held in Lyon, the union of the two churches was solemnly pro-claimed. The announcement, however, met with such stubborn opposition in Byzantium that the agreement could not be put into effect, and an even greater bitterness than formerly marked the relations between the emperor and the Pope. In 1281 Pope Martin IV went to the length of declaring the emperor a heretic and of forbidding Christian princes to communicate with him. Once again Christendom was split into opposing camps. Religious hatred was particularly strong in Sicily. On March 31, 1282, it flared up, causing a mutiny in Palermo, which quickly grew into a pitched battle. In the course of it so many lives were lost that the outbreak came to be known as the Sicilian Vespers.

With each passing decade the political difficulties besetting the Byzantines became more numerous and acute. The economic hardships and political quarrels increased, and religious sects multiplied even though Andronicus II repudi-ated the union of the two churches. Many took advantage of the peasants' poverty to encourage them to commit acts of violence, while the Turks made use of the confusion to establish themselves in Bithynia. Andronicus tried to check their advance by sending 10,000 mercenaries to fight them under the command of his co-emperor, Michael IX, but the campaign ended in failure. He made another attempt in 1304, this time using Roger de Flor and his Catalan troops for the purpose. They scored an early victory over the Turks but proceeded to celebrate it by plundering the country they had come to defend. Laden with booty, they withdrew to Gallipoli for the winter. The hatred they aroused resulted

108

in 1305 in the murder of Roger de Flor in the grounds of the imperial palace. Even then the Catalans did not disperse but continued to plunder Thrace for two more years.

Fighting dragged on in the Balkans and against the Italian merchant states; civil unrest continued, drawing fresh strength from the religious quarrels which divided the Byzantines at home and encouraged their enemies from abroad to attack them. By 1354 Serbia had conquered a good half of Byzantium's Balkan lands, Genoa had captured the island of Chios, and the Turks had crossed the Sea of Marmora, landed in Europe, and seized Gallipoli. Byzantium had lost so much territory that it hardly had the right to continue thinking of itself as a kingdom. In Asia it had been deprived of all its possessions, in Greece little remained apart from the hill town of Mistra in Sparta, and almost nothing survived in the Balkans. The emperor still held Thessalonica, most of Thrace, the islands in the north Aegean, and small areas of the Peloponnesus, but these possessions were so few, so scattered, and so weak that it was almost impossible for him to defend them. To all intents and purposes Byzantium now consisted of little more than Constantinople and the surrounding towns and villages. *Territorial losses*

The country's economic situation was disastrous. The people could not pay their taxes for lack of money or goods with which to do so. Constantinople's grain supplies had come from Thrace, but the war there had turned its farms into deserts. Imports had fallen off with the decline in Constantinople's trade; now most of the Eastern trade headed direct for the Italian merchant states, bypassing Constantinople, while the little that entered its port was controlled by the Genoese. The treasury was empty, and Empress Anne even had to pawn her jewels to the Venetians. Though they gave her only 30,000 ducats in return, she was never able to redeem them. They remained in Venice and found their way to the treasury of St. Mark's Church, where most of them are still to be found. In 1350 the Grand Duke of Muscovy sent a donation to the emperor in order that essential repairs might be carried out on the fabric of Hagia Sophia. He was greatly vexed when he learned that the emperor had used the money to enroll Moslem mercenaries in his army. In 1355 Constantinople, now synonymous with *Economic chaos*

Byzantium, was on the verge of collapse. The Latins had never ceased to regret the overthrow of the Latin Kingdom of Constantinople, and the Venetian Senate therefore began to debate, not how to save Constantinople from the Turks, but how to annex it before the Ottomans did so. Much credit must be given to the last emperors of Byzantium for their success in defending Constantinople from its enemies for the best part of another century.

The Emperor appeals for help
In 1355 Emperor John V appealed to Christendom for help. In return he assured the Pope that he would unite the two Churches, and he even offered to send his second son, Manuel, then aged little more than six, to Rome to be brought up as a Catholic. Pope Innocent VI's reply, though friendly enough in tone, contained no definite promise of help even though the Ottoman Sultan Murad I had by then invaded the Balkans. His seizure soon after of some Serbian territory did, however, result in a more sympathetic response to the Emperor's appeal in 1364 for help, for a call went out in the West for a Fifth Crusade. Its leader, King Peter of Cyprus, wanted it to be used to free his island; others were anxious for it to go to Byzantium's assistance; but it ended by sailing for Egypt.

In a desperate attempt to obtain help, John V set out for Hungary in 1366 in order personally to implore King Louis the Great to come to his aid. Failing to persuade him, the emperor proceeded to Rome in 1369. It was the first time in Byzantium's long history that her emperor had been reduced to the position of a supplicant, yet John returned to Constantinople in 1371 emptyhanded from his humiliating mission. Even the Turkish victory on the Maritsa shortly afterward over the Serbs failed to arouse the West, although it gave the Turks possession of Macedonia and reduced both the Byzantines and the Bulgarians almost to the position of vassals.

Battle of Kosovo
Things went from bad to worse. The battle fought by the Turks and the Serbians on the field of Kosovo in June, 1389, is an epic in Serbian history. Though the Ottoman Sultan Murad was killed in it, the Turkish victory put an end to Serbian independence and left Constantinople completely surrounded. The Turks continued to advance on all fronts, completely subjugating Bulgaria in 1393, capturing

Church of St. Catherine, Thessalonica, fourteenth century

Thessalonica in 1394, and invading Silistria by the end of the century.

It was with the consent of the Ottoman Sultan Bayazid, Murad's successor, that John v's throne later passed to Andronicus IV, then to John VII. These emperors could not avoid reigning as vassals of the Ottomans. Indeed, their situation was so desperate that Emperor Manuel II – a son of John v – decided personally to visit the West to obtain help. Leaving John VII, a son of Andronicus IV, in Constantinople to govern, he set out for Venice in December, 1399. After visiting some other Italian states, he went on to Paris and London. He was feted wherever he went, but no one came forward to promise to assist him in fighting the Turks. After three years spent in seeking aid, he failed to find a single ally.

He may perhaps have derived a little comfort from the news which reached him in Paris, when on his homeward journey, that Sultan Bayazid had been captured at Ankara in 1402 by the most successful warrior of his day, the terrifying Mongol Khan who is known to us as Tamerlane or Tamburlaine. Indeed, Tamerlane's victory did provide the Byzantines with a breathing space, for it reduced the Ottomans to a condition of utter confusion.

Byzantium doomed

But by then it was too late. The Byzantines were doomed. They were tired out, ruined, and pitifully few in number. The Byzantines lived on because Bayazid's sons were quarreling for his throne. The eldest, Suleiman, had seized his late father's Balkan lands and was fighting his brothers for the others. In return for their promise of help, Suleiman granted the Byzantines possession of Thessalonica, as well as of some coastal strips on the Aegean and the Black Sea, and freed them from the payment of tribute money.

Suleiman I (1403-11) kept these terms and so did his brother, Mohammed I (1413-21), but Murad II (1421-51) was unwilling to do so, and in 1422 he besieged Constantinople. Almost miraculously the town withstood the onslaught, but its inhabitants were never again to breathe with complete ease. John VIII (1425-48) ruled only over Constantinople and its districts; Byzantium's few remaining outposts on the Greek mainland and the Black Sea were now so completely cut off that they had passed into the hands of the emperor's brother and certain minor princes. John reigned in poverty, hard pressed on all sides by the Turks. He too appealed to the West for help, and in order to obtain it, he set out in November, 1437, to ask for it in person as his father and grandfather had done in the past. He was accompanied by one of his brothers, the Patriarch of Constantinople, seven metropolitans, numerous bishops, and a number of abbots, for he had decided to unite his church to the Catholic. In return for this, he hoped to obtain the aid he so greatly needed. He and his companions traveled

Union of the two Churches

to Ferrara, where the Council of the Churches was to meet in 1438 for the purpose. However, the Council's deliberations were so complicated and so lengthy that nothing had been achieved in the time set, and the conference was therefore transferred to Florence. Here, on July 6, 1439, the union of the two churches was at last proclaimed. The announcement was received with bitter resentment in Constantinople, and to this day the Orthodox Church refuses to recognize the union.

In Hungary, John Corvinus Hunyadi had met Ottoman onslaught with such a staunch resistance that the invaders found themselves in difficulties. The Pope called for a crusade to support him, and by the autumn of 1443, 25,000 Crusaders had met to fight the Ottomans under the command of Jagellon, King of Poland and Hungary, John Hunyadi, and the Serbian despot George Brankovic. They crossed the Danube, freed Sofia, and advanced on Thrace. Hopes rose when Sultan Murad suggested that peace talks should be held; then he suddenly changed his mind and launched a fresh attack. In November, 1444, he engaged the Crusaders in a battle on the shores of the Black Sea and destroyed them. Nevertheless, the Albanians rose against him, and in Greece, the Byzantine emperor's brother, Constantine, Despot of the Morea, steadfastly fought back. He carried off some minor successes in Boetia, but in 1446, Sultan Murad invaded Greece and besieged Constantinople.

He had acquired a new weapon of war, and although he *The first* had great faith in it, he was anxious to put it to the test. It *firearm* was a cannon, the first firearm to be used in the Eastern world; the size of its shot was small and the damage it caused was not disastrous, but it sufficed to confirm the hopes which the sultan placed on the cannon. Its psychological effect on the Byzantines probably contributed to the scale of the Ottoman victory. Yet although the Turks captured more than 60,000 prisoners in the campaign, they agreed to make peace in return for the payment of a heavy tribute. Two years later Constantine, Despot of the Morea, was therefore able to inherit the throne of his childless brother.

Constantine Paleologus (1449-53), who as a young man had used his mother's surname of Dragases, became emperor at a time when neither unflinching courage nor heroic determination could save Constantinople, the town that had once ruled an empire. Nevertheless, he tried to revive the union of the churches in the hope of obtaining in return help from the West and angered his few remaining subjects by his efforts. Even then Europe seemed blind to the danger presented by the Turks. The Latins, especially the King of Naples and Aragon, remained more anxious to obtain Constantinople for themselves than to defend it from the Ottomans and only the high-minded Genoese commander 113

H

Giovanni Giustiniani came to Constantine's help, bringing a force of Genoese soldiers with him. In 1451 Mohammed II, a young man of twenty-two, succeeded his father as sultan of the Ottoman Turks. His possessions encircled Constantinople, and he was not prepared to tolerate the existence of a Byzantine kernel in their midst. In preparation for the decisive encounter on which he had set his heart, he proceeded to build the large and imposing fortress of Rumeli Hissar on the Bosporus's European shore to serve as a springboard for one of his attacks. On April 1, 1453, he assumed personal command of the great army which he had assembled for the final battle for Constantinople. It outnumbered the defenders by some 20 to 1 and was supported by a large and powerful navy.

The beleaguered city was defended by a small Byzantine force aided by Giustiniani's 7,000 Latins and Genoese, as well as by its civilian population. Even so the enemy was relying on the damage to be done to the walls of Constantinople by a vast cannon supported by smaller cannons, all of which had been assembled and were in the charge of Western technicians serving the sultan as mercenaries. The Byzantines had no firearms and few resources, but they relied on God and their personal courage. On April 7 the Turks directed the muzzle of their largest cannon at the weakest spot in Constantinople's outer walls. Entry to the Golden Horn was still barred by a chain so that, on April 20, the naval battle was fought out on the Bosporus. The Byzantines had a mere handful of ships, and victory went to the Ottomans. They landed their ships the next day close to their new fortress of Rumeli Hissar. During the night they hauled them overland to the Golden Horn, along a causeway, and refloated them there before dawn in readiness to attack Constantinople's seawalls from that inlet. When the gallant defenders of Constantinople awoke on the morning of April 22 and found the Turkish vessels afloat there, they realized that their position was desperate, yet their courage and determination did not falter. Every able-bodied person from the emperor to the humblest shopkeeper, from the oldest to the youngest, took turns in defending the walls.

On May 29, after seven weeks of stubborn fighting, the
sultan launched the general attack, directing his main

effort against three gates, the Charisius or Adrianople Gate, the Pempton Gate, and the Gate of St. Romanus. The defenders saw that the end was at hand. They assembled in Hagia Sophia for a final service; then, after commending their souls to God, each went to his post. The emperor spent the night inspecting the defenses and encouraging and bidding farewell to his people. At dawn he too made his way to the point on the walls close to the Charisius Gate, which it had fallen to him to defend. The fighting was especially fierce near the Pempton and St. Romanus gates. The Turks attacked twice there and were twice repulsed, but Giustiniani was killed in the second attack, and on learning of his death, the Genoese troops lost heart. Then, while the Sultan's cannons pounded Constantinople's walls, the sultan called on his janissaries to carry out the third attack. Even now the defenders might have repulsed the finest troops in the Ottoman Army had not a little gate known as the Kirko Porta been left undefended and, according to some, unlocked. It was through that gate that the first janissaries penetrated into Constantinople; soon after, others poured into the city through the breached walls. They had to fight every inch of the way, for the defenders resisted savagely to the death. Constantine XI, the last Emperor of Byzantium, perished as gallantly as his heroic and loyal subjects. He died fighting at his post and his badly mutilated body was recognized only by the purple slippers covering his feet.

When Constantinople fell, Mohammed II, Fatih the Conqueror, as he was now called in honor of his victory, handed the vanquished town to his victorious troops to do with as they pleased during three days. They looted its treasures, massacred many of those who had survived the siege, and destroyed its largest churches. By the end of the third day the city had become a ruin, its beauty a memory. Little of value escaped the plunderers. Byzantium lay dead when the Sultan entered the city in triumph.

He proclaimed it the capital of the Ottoman Empire, and transformed the Christian Cathedral of Hagia Sophia into a mosque.

The fall of Constantinople

Epilogue: The Legacy of Byzantium

IN ancient times the Roman Empire embodied Europe; it alone represented it, and the only power that ever approached it in importance was Persia. Byzantium stepped into Rome's place, automatically assuming its high rank and reputation; to this was added a spiritual claim, that of the adoption of Christianity as the religion of the state. Although Armenia had adopted Christianity earlier (in 301), closely followed by Georgia, Byzantium held the position of the world's foremost Christian state for centuries to come and faced the great powers of the East as the only Christian state to rank as their equal. Even when Charlemagne challenged the Byzantine Emperor's supremacy in the West, he was successful only in the political sphere. In other respects Byzantium's reputation remained unaffected, and a couple of centuries later the Slavs were able to express the respect and universal admiration in which Byzantium continued to be held by referring to Constantinople as Tsargrad – meaning the capital of the Caesars and, as such, the capital of the world.

Although Constantinople's prestige suffered a setback during the Latin occupation (1204-61), it regained and retained it, at any rate until midway into the fourteenth century. Throughout the period it was universally regarded as the world's most cultured, civilized, and international city, for more people of different nationalities visited it yearly for religious, political, commercial, or cultural reasons than any other town including Rome.

Almost from its foundation till its death Constantinople served both to embody Christianity and to protect it, yet Europe never really understood or appreciated its importance as a bulwark against the East, especially against the

advance of Islam. Although the battle against Islam was

fought on the fringe of Europe and Asia during nine centuries, and although the whole of Byzantium was involved in the contest, the resistance stemmed from the capital, from Constantinople. The Christian civilization which forms the basis of our culture and way of life not only was developed and established in Byzantium, but was defended there, and this made it possible for it to take firm root in the West. But for Byzantium, the character of European civilization would have been very different from what it is and so would most of our traditions and everyday customs.

Constantinople's wealth, and through it that of the Byzantine state, flowed chiefly from its trade, its splendor stemmed from its emperors and their court, its significance from the taste, industry, and skill of its large and mixed population, but it derived its authority from the willingness with which the Byzantines devoted their genius and their resources to glorifying God, their intellectual gifts to civilizing the world, and their artistry to rendering it beautiful. Their creativeness overflowed from the religious to the secular sphere to create a civilization of outstanding quality, unity, and forcefulness.

The importance of that civilization was so much appreciated in Europe that in the Middle Ages people came to believe that wisdom and learning really came from the East. That idea was partly based on the number and importance of the theological works produced in Byzantium, but it was also due to the fact that many of the works which had been written by ancient Greeks reached Europe in transcriptions made by Byzantine scribes, not in the form of earlier Greek manuscripts.

Yet Europe was not indebted to Byzantium only for religious texts and for many fine examples of early Greek literature and philosophy, or even for its conception of kingship and coronation ceremonial. Europe also owed much of its knowledge of banking, economics, commerce, and military and diplomatic tactics to the Byzantines. Justinian's legal code still influences many aspects of European law, while the works of Byzantine geographers told Europeans a good deal about the nature of the world. Similarly Byzantium's position as commercial middleman between East and

West helped bring the continents into direct touch. Yet the influence exercised by Byzantium on the Slav nations and also on Greece – which considers itself Byzantium's heir – has proved of even wider significance since, by providing these countries with its own form of Christianity, Byzantium also molded their outlooks and their cultures.

The importance of Byzantium's educational contribution to the West, though great in itself, is outmatched by its artistic legacy. St. Mark's Cathedral in Venice is a copy of the Byzantine church of the Holy Apostles in Constantinople, yet centuries earlier, Byzantium had already provided the West with the dome and the cruciform plan, a type of church which has come to typify Christianity. The influence of Byzantine art abroad was at all times very considerable. At the end of the seventh century the Ommayad caliphs turned to Byzantium for the superb glass mosaic decorations which still adorn the Dome of the Rock in Jerusalem and the Great Mosque in Damascus; Byzantine art dictated the form and styles of the Christian arts of the Slavonic world; it became for the primitive painters of Italy the springboard for their religious art; it was adopted in Sicily; it penetrated to France, Germany and England; it left its mark wherever Christian art was taking root – indeed, its effects are still to be seen in the work of many of the most outstanding painters of today, notably Georges Rouault.

The impact which Byzantine artists made on their contemporaries can be ascribed, at any rate in part, to their appreciation of beauty in all its forms. They loved to see handsome people dressed in lovely clothes and adorned with exquisite jewelry, living in splendid houses furnished with fine silks and admirably designed objects, surrounded by lovely gardens laid out in beautiful settings. They delighted in the splendor and diversity of nature. They expressed these tastes with great forcefulness and sincerity in the religious works they created, but their delight was tinged with the knowledge that their pleasure in these things was temporary; paradise alone could provide permanent joy. Their recognition of the difficulty of gaining admittance to paradise is perhaps responsible for the touch of sadness, of otherworldness in their art – an element which contributes greatly to the art's appeal.

From the sixth to the mid-fourteenth century – a period of some 800 years – they surrounded themselves with all that was most sumptuous, exquisite, and splendid. As a result, during those years Constantinople outshone Venice when the Republic was at the height of its prosperity, Florence when enshrined in the glory of the Italian Renaissance, Paris in the nineteenth century when its reputation was at its height. Until the Latin conquest travelers looked on Constantinople as the sovereign city; in the eyes of Christendom it was also a holy city, often even the holiest of cities.

Chronology of the Emperors of Byzantium

Dynasty of Constantine
Constantine I (the Great)
   324–37
Constantius 337–61
   Sole emperor 353–61
Julian 361–63

Intermediary Dynasty
Jovian 363–64
Valens 364–78

Dynasty of Theodosius
Theodosius I (the Great)
   379–95
Arcadius 395–408
Theodosius II 408–50
Marcian 450–57

Dynasty of Leo
Leo I 457–74
Leo II 474
Zeno 474–91
Basilicus 475–76
Anastasius I
   491–518

Dynasty of Justinian
Justin I 518–27
Justinian I (the Great)
   527–65
Justin II 565–78
Tiberius I 578–82
Maurice 582–602

Phocas (the Usurper)
   602–10

Dynasty of Heraclius
Heraclius 610–41
Constantine III and
   Heraclonas 641
Constans II 641–68
Constantine IV Pogonatus
   668–85
Justinian II Rhinotmetus
   685–95 and again 705–11
Leontius (usurper)
   695–98
Tiberius II 698–705
Philippicus Bardanes
   (nondynastic) 711–13
Anastasius II (nondynastic)
   713–15
Theodosius III
   (nondynastic) 715–17

Dynasty of Isaurians
Leo III 717–41
Constantine V Copronymus
   741–75
Leo IV (husband of
   Empress Irene) 775–80
Constantine VI (Irene's
   son) 780–97
Irene 797–802

Nicephorus I (usurper)
802–11
Stauracius (usurper) 811
Michael I Rhangabe
(husband of Empress
Procopia) 811–13
Leo V (the Armenian –
usurper) 813–20

*Dynasty of Amorians or
Phrygians*
Michael II (the
Stammerer) 820–29
Theophilus 829–42
Michael III (the
Drunkard) 842–67

Dynasty of Macedonians
Basil I 867–86
Leo VI (the Wise) 886–912
Alexander 912–13
Constantine VII
Porphyrogenitus 913–59
Romanus Lecapenus
(co-ruler) 920–44
Romanus II 959–63
Nicephorus II Phocas
(usurper) 963–9
John I Tzimisces (usurper)
969–76

*Dynasty of Macedonians
Return to Power*
Basil II Bulgaroctonus
(Bulgar Slayer)
976–1025
Constantine VIII 1025–28
Romanus III Argyrus
(husband of the
Empress Zoe) 1028–34
Michael IV the
Paphlagonian (second

husband of the Empress
Zoe) 1034–41
Michael V Calaphates
1041–42
Zoe and Theodora 1042
Constantine IX
Monomachus 1042–55
Theodora 1055–56
Michael VI Stratioticus
(nondynastic 1056–57

Dynasty of the Dukas
Isaac I Comnenus 1057–59
Constantine X Ducas
1059–67
Romanus IV Diogenes
1068–71
Michael VII Dukas
Parapinakes 1071–78
Nicephorus III
Botaneiates 1078–81

Dynasty of the Comnenes
Alexius I Comnenus
1081–1118
John II 1118–43
Manuel I Comnenus
1143–80
Alexius II Comnenus
1180–83
Andronicus I Comnenus
1183–85

Dynasty of the Angeli
Isaac II Angelus 1185–95
and again 1203–4
Alexius Angelus III
1195–1203
Isaac II and Alexius
Angelus IV 1203–4
Alexius V Ducas
Murtzuphlus (Usurper)
1204

Latin Rulers of
Constantinople
Baldwin I of Flanders
1204–5
Henry of Flanders
1206–16
Peter of Courtenay 1217
Yolande 1217–19
Robert of Courtenay
1221–28
Baldwin II 1228–61

Byzantine Rulers of
Nicaean Empire
Theodore I Lascaris
1204–22
John III Ducas Vatatzes
1222–54
Theodore II Lascaris
1254–58
John IV Lascaris 1258–61

Dynasty of the Paleologi
Michael VIII Paleologus
1259–82

Andronicus II Paleologus
1282–1328
Michael IX Paleologus
1294–1320
Andronicus III Paleologus
1328–41
John V Paleologus
1341–91
John VI Cantacuzenus
(usurper) 1347–54
Andronicus IV Paleologus
1376–79
John VII Paleologus
1390
Manuel II Paleologus
1391–1425
John VIII Paleologus
1425–48
Constantine XI Paleologus
1449–53

Table of Main Dates

THE EAST	THE WEST
324 Ascession of Constantine the Great, sole ruler of the Roman Empire	306 Constantine installed as his father's successor in York
325 First Council of the Churches held at Nicaea	313 Christianity legalized
330 Dedication of Constantinople	
	407 Roman legions withdraw from Britain
	454 Death of Attila, the Hun
550–1 First war against Slavs fought on the Danube	455 Vandals sack Rome
	493–555 Ostrogoth kingdom in Italy
576–82 Intermittent Avar and Slav raids on Byzantium	560 Avars found a kingdom that endures till mid-seventh century
	568–600 Langobards conquer Italy
592–602 Byzantines campaign against Slavs	c. 570–632 Mohammed, founder of Islam
604–20 Persian war with Persian capture of Jerusalem in 614	572 Visigoths start on conquest of Spain
	590–604 Reign of Pope Gregory the Great
634–42 Arabs conquer Byzantium's eastern territories	
673–77 Arabs attack Constantinople	614 Slavs settle in Dalmatia
	711–14 Arabs conquer Spain
713 Bulgars besiege Constantinople	
717–18 Arabs besiege Constantinople	768–814 Life of Charlemagne
	800 Charlemagne crowned

726 Start of Iconoclast
Controversy
730 Iconoclast ban imposed
756 and 763 Successful wars
against Bulgars

804–14 King Krum of
Bulgaria attacks
Byzantium
843 Lifting of Iconoclast
ban

1054 Separation of the two
Churches

1071 Battle of Manzikert

1097 Seljuks defeated at
Dorylaeum

1187 Saladin captures
Jerusalem

1204 Latin Kingdom of
Constantinople.
Establishment of Kingdoms
of Nicaea and Trebizond
1219–21 Mongols march
on Persia
1220–1353 Mongols rule
Persia

1267 Genoese take over
district of Galata in
Constantinople
1282 Sicilian Vespers

1358 Turks appear at walls of
Constantinople

1373 John v reigns as
vassal of Sultan Murad i

1394 Turks besiege
Constantinople

Emperor of the West by
the Pope in Rome
Early in ninth century Arabs
appear in Sicily and
southern Italy

862–912 Life of Oleg, Prince
of Kiev
871–99 Reign of Alfred, King
of England
896 Magyars reach the
Danube from Asia
907 The Rhos attack
Constantinople
911 Norman kingdom of
France
951 Otto i of Germany
conquers Lombards and
marches on Sicily
959–75 Reign of Edgar,
King of Anglo-Saxons
988 Kievan Rus adopts
Orthodox Christianity
1000 Establishment of
Kingdom of Hungary
1030–91 Normans conquer
Southern Italy and Sicily

1066 Normans conquer
England

1077–1307 Seljuk
Sultanate of Iconium
1086 Domesday Book
1096 First Crusade,
captures Jerusalem in 1099

1130 Kingdom of Two
Sicilies
1147–9 Second Crusade
1154–89 Henry Plantagenet
king of England
1152–90 Reign of Frederick i
Barbarossa, Emperor of
Germany

1422 Turks besiege
Constantinople
1439 Union of the two
Churches proclaimed in
Florence

1453 Capture of
Constantinople by the
Turks ends the existence
of Byzantium

1180 Serbian Kingdom
established by Stephen
Nemanja
1186 Second Bulgarian
Kingdom

1189–92 Third Crusade
1201–04 Fourth Crusade

1222 Mongols appear in
Europe

1300 Ottoman Turks enter
Asia Minor
1308 Ottomans land in
Europe
1327–77 Edward III king
of England
1337–1453 Hundred Years
War
1351 Tamerlane conquers
Persia

1360–89 Murad I Sultan of
Ottoman Turks

1389–1403 Bayazid I Sultan
of Ottoman Turks
1389 Battle of Kosovo
ends existence of Serbian
Kingdom

1413–21 Mohammed I
Sultan of Ottoman Turks
1421–51 Murad II Sultan
of Ottoman Turks

1451–81 Mohammed II,
Fatih, the Conqueror
Sultan of Ottoman Turks

1492 Christopher Columbus
discovers America

Suggestions for Further Reading

Beckwith, John, *The Art of Constantinople*, 2nd ed. Phaidon, 1968

Byron, R., *The Byzantine Achievement*. Russell, 1929

Cambridge Medieval History, J. M. Hussey and others, eds. Vol. 4, Part 1, 1966; Part 2, 1967

Comnena, Anna, *Alexiad of the Princess Anna Comnena*, E. A. Dawes, trans. Barnes & Noble, 1967

Dalton, O. M., *Byzantine Art and Archaeology*. Dover, 1961

Hussey, J., *The Byzantine World*, 2nd ed. Hillary, 1961

Ostrogorsky, G., *History of the Byzantine State*. Rutgers University Press, 1958

Psellus, M., *Fourteen Byzantine Rulers*. Penguin Books, 1966

Runciman, S., *Byzantine Civilisation*. St Martin's, 1933

Talbot Rice, D., *Byzantine Art,* rev. ed. Penguin Books, 1968. *Byzantine Painting: The Last Phase*. Dial, 1968 *The Byzantines*. Thames and Hudson, 1962

Talbot Rice, T., *Everyday Life in Byzantium*. Putnam, 1967

Index